MUSIC
THEORY

BY BARRETT TAGLIARINO

A POCKET REFERENCE GUIDE
FOR ALL MUSICIANS

HAL•LEONARD•

ISBN 978-1-4234-3587-7

HAL•LEONARD®
CORPORATION
7777 W. BLUEMOUND RD. P.O. BOX 13819 MILWAUKEE, WI 53213

In Australia contact:
Hal Leonard Australia Pty. Ltd.
4 Lentara Court
Cheltenham, Victoria, 3192 Australia
Email: ausadmin@halleonard.com.au

Visit Hal Leonard Online at
www.halleonard.com

CONTENTS

INTRODUCTION

Welcome to the study of music theory. Getting a grasp of the basic concepts presented in this book will help you open up a world of possibilities in composition, improvisation, and comprehension of the universal language of music.

As in any art form, theory is the study of principles observed from actual works. We'll recognize customary practices such as common chord progressions, but there are no rules in music. For example, any chord may be followed by any other chord. If it sounds good, it's right! The only "wrong" notes are the ones you don't like! Never mind the old adage that learning theory will stifle your creativity in some way. It's merely a means by which you are adding to what you already know, assigning names to familiar sounds, and allowing yourself to express new ones—verbally or written—to other musicians.

This is an introductory text for beginners and by-ear players who want to start organizing their musical thoughts. We'll cover the essentials you need to get started: basic notation, ear training, and the building blocks of scales and harmony. With these mastered, you'll be better equipped to tackle other facets of this broad subject. Excluding technique, theory encompasses all musical topics, including improvisation, composition, orchestration, analysis, and style.

Earlier lessons in this book must be mastered before beginning subsequent ones. It's important to pace yourself; work with it consistently, but in short time frames. If too much time passes between study sessions, you'll forget what you've learned and will have trouble moving forward. Conversely, it's easy to become overloaded if you cover too much in one session. The resulting frustration can throw off your study habits, especially if you are working on your own, outside a classroom.

Work with this book at least three or four times per week, but always for an hour or less at a time. If you have more time, opt for more short sessions rather than fewer long ones. This goes against human nature a bit, so create a practice schedule and log your time to keep your sessions under control.

The written exercises and ear-training drills are here to help you apply what you're learning. While you may understand a lesson on an intellectual level in fairly short order, you'll need a lot of practice before it becomes second nature when applying it. This is normal, especially in music. It means you should continue to practice previously covered areas and create your own exercises in a similar fashion to those presented, while slowly progressing through the new material.

You can expect the various areas covered in this book to internally develop at different speeds, depending on your experience. For instance, those who have spent many hours of their lives singing—but not sight reading—will have to spend more time on the written exercises. Those who have only read music on an instrument may need to spend more time on the ear-training drills.

BASICS

Rhythm is the timing of when sound starts and stops. *Pitch* is heard as a high or low sound created by the vibrations of an instrument at a fast or slow frequency, respectively. *Harmony* is produced by combining simultaneous pitches.

We'll refer to the piano keyboard for convenient study of pitch-related concepts, but everything you'll learn applies to all pitched instruments.

The Musical Alphabet

Pitches are named using the first seven letters of the alphabet: A–B–C–D–E–F–G. The sound itself is a *tone*, while the name or symbol is a *note*; however, these two words are sometimes used interchangeably. When two tones musically sound similar, we give them the same letter name.

The two A notes below are said to be an *octave* (a distance of eight letters/notes) apart.

Octave
A B C D E F G A
1 2 3 4 5 6 7 8

The seven letters repeat to include all possible pitches, from the lowest foghorn to the highest dog whistle, and beyond. As you reach G, the letters start over again with A, and so on…

A B C D E F G / A B C D E F G / A B C…

It will make things easier if you also memorize the musical alphabet backwards, going down in pitch on the keyboard.

GFEDCBA/GFE...

EXERCISE I

Recite the musical alphabet aloud, starting from each letter and completing three octaves. Here are two examples to get you started.

ABCDEFG/ABCDEFG/ABCDEFG/A
BCDEFGA/BCDEFGA/BCDEFGA/B

Now, recite the alphabet backwards. Again, practice with all seven possible starting letters.

GFEDCBA/GFEDCBA/GFEDCBA/G
FEDCBAG/FEDCBAG/FEDCBAG/F

Counting

Nearly all music contains a recurring beat (or *pulse*) that serves as a background against which the rhythms (start times and durations) of notes are measured. It's vitally important that this beat be felt in your body and present in the back of your mind when you play music or listen to it critically. For this, we must practice tapping our feet while counting. Count aloud (don't just mumble it—make it loud!) along with the CD track while tapping the toe end of your foot on the floor.

We can count up to any number of beats before starting over. Usually a pattern of strong and weak beats can be felt in the music, indicating the easiest way to count it. The strongest beat is called beat 1 (the *downbeat*) of the pattern. In songs, counting to four is the most common grouping, though there are many others. The booming bass drum is often played on beats 1 and 3, while the snare drum snaps on 2 and 4 (the *backbeats*).

Bar lines separate the groups of beats. Each group is called a *measure* (or *bar*). A *double bar line* is used to end a song or section. Here we have a four-measure section of music.

bar line   double bar line

1 2 3 4 | 1 2 3 4 | 1 2 3 4 | 1 2 3 4

EXERCISE 2

Practice counting four-beat measures aloud while tapping your foot. Do this a few minutes each day until the skill becomes relaxed and easy. Tap along with a metronome at a slow setting to help yourself learn to keep steady time. You'll need your sense of the beat to be automatic, firmly ingrained in your mind so that later you can accurately perform other rhythms in relation to it. You'll know you're getting it when you can keep your foot tapping evenly with a metronome while carrying on a conversation.

EXERCISE 3

In addition to keeping a steady beat, you'll also
need to find beat 1, the strongest beat of the
measure, after hearing music for just a few beats.
Develop this skill by counting aloud along with
recordings in your collection. Stop counting and
talk about something else for a few seconds as the
song plays, then return your attention to the
music and start counting again as soon as you can
feel where you are in relation to the downbeat
(beat 1).

The Staff

Pitch and rhythm are both written on a *staff* consisting of
five lines and four spaces.

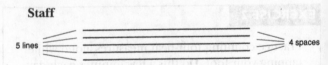

Each line and each space on the staff represents a different pitch. The pitches are defined by the *clef*, a symbol
placed at the beginning of the first staff of a musical
piece.

There are several different clefs, each suited for the pitch
ranges of various instruments. The *treble* or "**G**" clef
shown below is the most commonly used clef. The lower
loop of the clef encircles the second line, which is the
note G.

Treble or G Clef

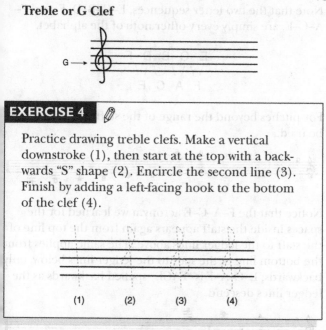

EXERCISE 4

Practice drawing treble clefs. Make a vertical downstroke (1), then start at the top with a backwards "S" shape (2). Encircle the second line (3). Finish by adding a left-facing hook to the bottom of the clef (4).

(1)   (2)   (3)   (4)

Once the note G is defined on the staff, all the others fall into place.

The **lines** on the treble clef are E–G–B–D–F (**E**very **G**ood **B**oy **D**oes **F**ine). The **spaces** on the treble clef spell the word "FACE."

Note that the two letter sequences, E–G–B–D–F and F–A–C–E, are simply every other note of the alphabet.

For pitches beyond the range of the staff, *ledger lines* must be used.

Notice that the F–A–C–E acronym we learned for the spaces inside the staff appears again from the top line of the staff to the ledger lines above. The same applies from the bottom line of the staff to the ledger lines below, only backwards; E–C–A–F is "FACE" spelled backwards as the ledger lines descend.

Notice that the *bass clef* is also called the "**F**" clef because two dots surround the pitch F on the fourth line. From here, we can see that the lines of the bass clef are G–B–D–F–A, which we can remember as "**G**ood **B**oys **D**o **F**ine **A**lways." The spaces are A–C–E–G, which we can remember as "**A**ll **C**ows **E**at **G**rass."

Bass or F Clef

ll Cows Eat Grass is found on the ledger lines above and
elow the bass staff, too.

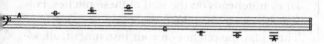

Notes

ll notes have *heads*. The head should be a slanted oval,
milar to a letter "O," that fits exactly on a space or line.

EXERCISE 5

Practice drawing noteheads in the **spaces**. Be
careful—don't make them too big or too small.

Now, draw noteheads on the **lines**, like the one
provided. You should be able to see the hollow
part of the head even though the line cuts
through it.

The position of the notehead on the staff deter-
mines its pitch.

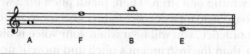

15

EXERCISE 6

Draw noteheads on the staff at these pitches. Follow the clef to find the correct line or space. Then play the pitches on your instrument, allowing four foot taps for each. If the pitches are outside of your instrument's range, play them in a higher or lower octave.

B E C D F A E G

E A F D B C G B

Ear Training

This is a vital subject that every musician should regularly practice. Singing is critical to developing your musicianship, even if you don't like your voice or are self-conscious. Using an instrument alone will not be enough; singing produces much faster results in your ear training.

Start by singing *any* tone (just say a single syllable such as "hey" and hold it), then make it go up and down like a slide whistle or a siren. Then, play a pitch on a well-tuned keyboard instrument (preferably) and try to match it. With practice, you will hear when your voice is higher or lower than the instrument's pitch and move it up and down accordingly.

Repeat this exercise daily using random pitches on an instrument. Don't progress to other ear-training drills involving pitch until your pitch-matching skill is fairly consistent. If you've tried for awhile and you're not sure if you're hitting the notes, it's a good idea to consult a voice teacher.

If you feel you need additional ear training practice material, a great idea is to create your own. Write out some easy examples that use the ear training skill you're currently working on, making the written answer key first. Random notes and rhythms are fine; it's not a composition. Then record yourself carefully playing the examples several times in a row, announcing each one before you play it. Take a break, then play back and transcribe each example, and check it against your key.

The Grand Staff

A treble and bass clef will often be used jointly for a wider range of notes. The two staves are joined with a *brace*, resulting in a *grand staff*.

Grand Staff

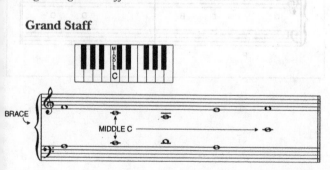

On the grand staff, the first ledger line below the treble clef is the same note as the first ledger line above the bass clef. This pitch is *middle C*, located in the middle of the piano keyboard.

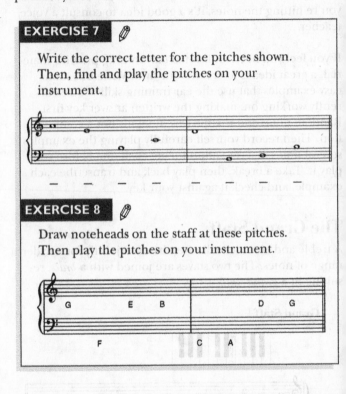

EXERCISE 7

Write the correct letter for the pitches shown.
Then, find and play the pitches on your
instrument.

EXERCISE 8

Draw noteheads on the staff at these pitches.
Then play the pitches on your instrument.

G   E   B   D   G

F   C   A

RHYTHM

A note has two rhythmic parts: *attack* (when it begins) and *duration* (how long it lasts).

Note Values

The more stuff a notehead has attached to it, the shorter the note's duration. Let's look at the different types of notes, from long to short.

A hollow notehead without *stems* or *flags* is a *whole note*. It sustains for four beats. Tap your foot and count to four while letting a C note ring on your instrument. Stop the note on beat 1 of the next measure.

Whole Notes

A hollow notehead with a stem is a *half note*. This note rings out for two beats. Two half notes occupy four beats, the same amount of time as one whole note. Tap and count while playing these notes on beats 1 and 3. Again, use a C note on your instrument.

Half Notes

Notice that although the notes are evenly spaced over the numbers, the attack, or start time, of the second note is really determined by the duration of the note preceding it. The second note starts on beat 3 because the first note was two full beats in length.

Stem Direction

When a stemmed note is on or above the center line of the staff, its stem hangs down from the left side of the notehead.

Stemmed Notes on or above the Center Line

If the note is on or below the center line, its stem points up from the right side of the notehead.

Stemmed Notes on or below the Center Line

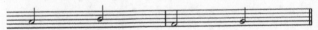

Stemmed notes on the center line should point in the same direction as their neighbors.

EXERCISE 9

Draw stems to make half notes on the heads below using correct stem direction. Stems should be straight and approximately one octave long.

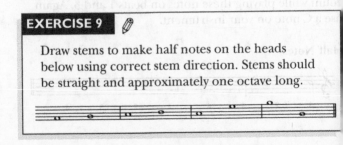

The rules of correct notation may seem a bit picky, but by making it look neat and accurate, the music will be easier to read.

For a *quarter note*, draw a filled-in head with a stem. This note lasts for one beat. Tap your foot, count aloud, and play the note C on each beat (number).

Quarter Notes

EXERCISE 10

Practice drawing quarter notes for the pitches below. Follow the same rule for stem direction as with half notes.

The next, smaller rhythmic value is an *eighth note*, created by adding a flag to the stem. The flag should look like a real flag, curving away, then pointing back at the note-head. Regardless of stem direction, the flag always goes to the right.

There are two eighth notes in one beat. To count them, insert the word "and" between the numbers, like this: "*1 and, 2 and, 3 and, 4 and…*" Your foot should reach its highest point just as you say the word "and."

Eighth Notes

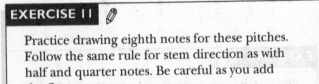

EXERCISE 11 🖉

Practice drawing eighth notes for these pitches. Follow the same rule for stem direction as with half and quarter notes. Be careful as you add the flags.

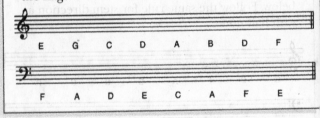

E   G   C   D   A   B   D   F

F   A   D   E   C   A   F   E

This pyramid shows the relationships between various note durations that work across all divisions of time. For instance, two eighths equal one quarter; two quarter notes plus one half note equal one whole note, etc.

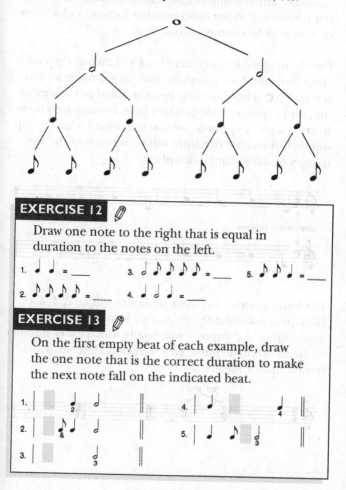

EXERCISE 12

Draw one note to the right that is equal in duration to the notes on the left.

1. ♩ ♩ = ____ 3. ♩ ♪ ♪ ♪ ♪ = ____ 5. ♪ ♪ ♩ = ____

2. ♪ ♪ ♪ ♪ = ____ 4. ♩ ♩ ♩ = ____

EXERCISE 13

On the first empty beat of each example, draw the one note that is the correct duration to make the next note fall on the indicated beat.

1. | ♩ ♩ ||
   2

2. | ♪ ♩ ♩ ||
   &

3. | ♩ ||
   3

4. | ♪ ♩ ||
   4

5. | ♩ ♪ ♩ ||
   3

Meter

The number of beats in each measure is called the *meter*, and is indicated at the beginning of the music with a *time signature*. The top number indicates the number of beats per measure, and the lower number indicates which type of note is to be counted as one beat.

On the next page is an example of 4/4 meter, also called "four-four time" or "common time." It's sometimes written with a **C**. There are four beats counted in each measure, and a quarter note gets one beat. Immediately upon hearing a piece of music, we can usually tell what the top number of its time signature will be because of the frequency of the strongest downbeat.

common time signature

The lower number in a time signature will be 2, 4, 8, or 16. This is not instantly discernible from hearing the music alone. A composer will decide which lower number to use to make the music easy to count. Here are some commonplace meters.

"cut" time

EXERCISE 14

Draw bar lines on the example below to make it equal 4/4 time.

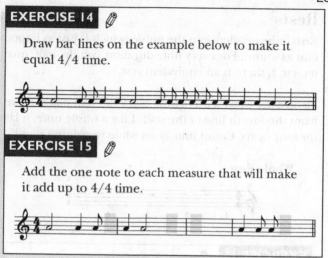

EXERCISE 15

Add the one note to each measure that will make it add up to 4/4 time.

Pickups

Once a meter is set, the notes in each measure must add up to exactly the number of beats it specifies. The exception to this rule is the first measure, which may contain fewer beats than the time signature specifies. When this happens, the first measure is called a *pickup measure*. The notes themselves are called *pickup notes*.

Rests

Rests indicate silence in the music, which is just as important as sound. For every note duration (whole, half, quarter, etc.), there is an equivalent rest.

Picture the *whole rest* as a little black hat that hangs down from the fourth line of the staff. Like a whole note, it lasts for four beats. Count four beats while remaining silent.

Whole Rest

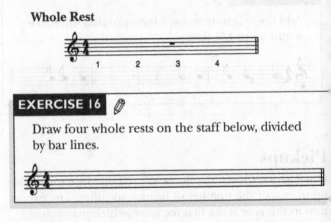

EXERCISE 16 ✏

Draw four whole rests on the staff below, divided by bar lines.

The *half rest* is also a black hat, but it stands upright from the third line. Think of the half rest as being lighter in weight than the whole rest, so it stands upright instead of hanging down. The half rest is two beats in length.

Half Rests

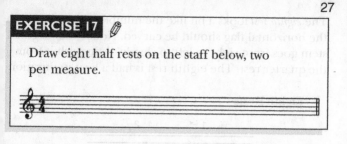

EXERCISE 17 ✏

Draw eight half rests on the staff below, two per measure.

Like the quarter note, a *quarter rest* is one beat in length.

Quarter Rest

A professionally engraved quarter rest looks like a cursive "W" placed sideways on the staff (≹).

When hand-writing them, it's best to keep it simple, as follows:

1. Make a diagonal line from left to right through the center line.
2. Draw a counterclockwise hook at the bottom.
3. Add a counterclockwise hook at the top.

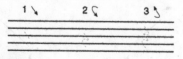

EXERCISE 18 ✏

Draw four evenly-spaced quarter rests in each measure below.

The *eighth rest* looks a bit like the number seven, although the horizontal flag should be curved. Notice the diagonal stem goes from right to left to clearly distinguish it from the quarter rest. The eighth rest is half a beat in duration.

Eighth Rests

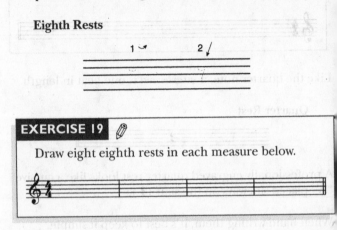

EXERCISE 19

Draw eight eighth rests in each measure below.

Review the pyramid of rest equivalents. Name each aloud.

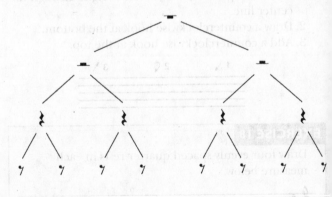

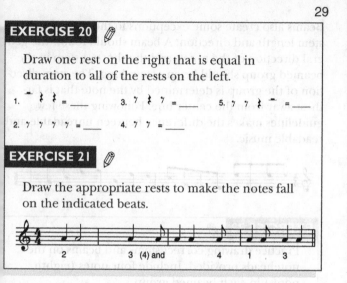

EXERCISE 20

Draw one rest on the right that is equal in duration to all of the rests on the left.

1. ▬ 𝄽 𝄽 = _____   3. 𝄾 𝄽 𝄾 = _____   5. 𝄾 𝄾 𝄽 ▬ = _____

2. 𝄾 𝄾 𝄾 𝄾 𝄾 = _____   4. 𝄾 𝄾 = _____

EXERCISE 21

Draw the appropriate rests to make the notes fall on the indicated beats.

Beams

When multiple eighth notes appear in sequence, *beams* are used instead of individual flags. Beaming makes eighth notes easier to read and write.

There are some important rules about beaming. In 4/4 time, a beam should not cross beat 3. Instead, draw two beamed groups. Imagine a line dividing the measure in half.

Beams also create some exceptions to the rules about stem length and direction. A beam should follow the general direction of the notes, and the shortest stem in the beamed group should be an octave long. The stem direction of the group is determined by the note that is farthest away from the center line. Following these few guidelines makes the difference between unreadable and readable music.

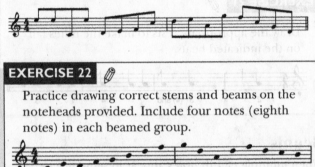

EXERCISE 22

Practice drawing correct stems and beams on the noteheads provided. Include four notes (eighth notes) in each beamed group.

EXERCISE 23 🖉

Rewrite this example, following correct stem-direction and beaming rules, including showing beats 1 and 3.

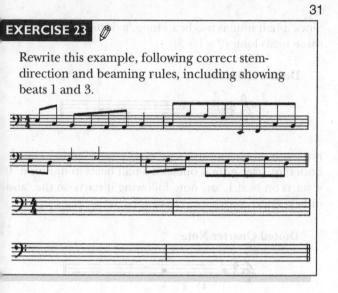

Dots

A *dot* added after any note or rest increases its duration by one half of its original value. For instance, if a note is four beats long, the same note with a dot after it is now six beats long (4 + 2 = 6).

Dotted Whole Note

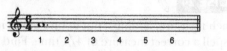

32

Since a half note is two beats long, a dotted half note is three beats long $(2 + 1 = 3)$.

Dotted Half Note

For a dotted quarter note, we must count "ands." The dotted quarter note is one-and-a-half beats in duration. If it starts on beat 1, any note following it starts on the "and" of beat 2.

Dotted Quarter Note

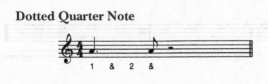

Tap, count, and play (or sing) along with this example, which uses dotted notes.

EXERCISE 24

In each measure, adding a dot to one of the notes will spell a correct measure of 4/4 time. Find the note and add the dot to it. (The notes are spaced incorrectly on purpose, to confuse you.)

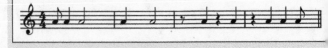

Ties

Consider the dotted whole note for a minute. It is six beats in duration, longer than a measure of 4/4 time. In fact, it is not uncommon for one pitch to sustain for several measures. However, for ease of reading, there should always be something written on beat 1 of each measure.

To correctly notate duration longer than a measure, *ties* are used. When notes are tied, only the first one is struck. Its duration is then extended by the value of the other note(s) tied to it. Here is a whole note in one measure tied to a half note in the next measure. A half rest completes the second measure. The pitch sounds for six beats, while two measures of 4/4 time are counted.

Note the difference between a tie and a *slur*, which is used to show a smooth connection between notes of different pitch.

Since rests are silent, we never use ties to join them. We also do not use dots with whole, half, or quarter rests in 4/4 time. Like the example below, use the correct number and type of rests needed to create the necessary duration of silence, so that any notes that follow fall on the desired beat.

Along with correct beaming, ties are also used to make beats easy to see within a measure. If eighth notes are present in a measure, imagine a line between beats 2 and 3 that notes or rests may not cross; there should be something written on beat 3 for us to read. If a sustained note from a previous beat is desired, it is tied to a note on beat 3.

When considering the best way to write a note, try to create the necessary duration by using the smallest number of symbols on the page, while still showing beat 1, and showing beat 3 if eighth notes or rests are present.

1. Use one large note if possible.
2. Add a dot if needed to complete the necessary duration.
3. If the note extends past the bar line, use a tie instead of a dot.
4. If there are eighth notes in the measure, use a tie across the imaginary bar line before beat 3.

Tap, count, and play (or sing) along with this example, which uses dotted and tied notes.

EXERCISE 25 ✏

Rewrite this example using correct
rhythmic notation.

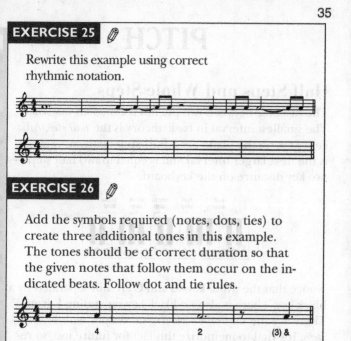

EXERCISE 26 ✏

Add the symbols required (notes, dots, ties) to
create three additional tones in this example.
The tones should be of correct duration so that
the given notes that follow them occur on the indicated beats. Follow dot and tie rules.

PITCH

Half Steps and Whole Steps

The distance between two pitches is called an *interval*. The smallest interval in basic theory is the *half step*. Adjacent keys on the piano are a half step apart. A *whole step* is the next larger interval and is equal to two half steps—a two-key distance on the keyboard.

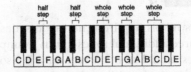

Notice that the white keys B and C are not separated by a black key. There is also no black key separating E from F. These are the *naturally-occurring* or, simply, *natural half steps*. It's vital to memorize this fact for future use, so repeat it aloud.

"There are natural half steps from B to C and from E to F."

While the natural half steps are fairly easy to locate on an instrument, we have to remember them when looking at a staff.

Natural Half Steps

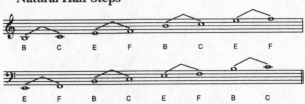

Sharps, Flats, and Naturals

Although pitches are named using only seven letters of
the alphabet (A through G), a complete octave is divided
into twelve tones.

We only use a seven-letter musical alphabet because most
songs are based on seven-note scales. A scale can be
spelled quickly by using all seven letters. Some of the letters may have *accidental* symbols (♯, ♭, or ♮) after them to
show exactly which of the twelve possible notes is desired.
Accidentals are of vital importance, so repeat this sen-
tence aloud.

> *"The sharp (♯) raises a note, the flat (♭) lowers a note,
> and the natural (♮) puts it back."*

The main part of the accidental symbol should be about
the size of a notehead and as close as possible to the notehead without crashing into it.

EXERCISE 27 🖉

Practice drawing the three accidental types on
line and space notes. The flat symbol should have
a point at the bottom.

An important term for a scale note is *diatonic*, meaning "from the scale." Diatonic is also used to describe chords and melodies that are based on a scale. There are seven diatonic notes in a scale, leaving five *non-diatonic* (or non-scale) notes within the one-octave range. This is reflected in the design of the piano keyboard. The white keys form a C major scale. In between the white keys are five black keys. The white keys are said to be diatonic to the C major scale. The black keys are non-diatonic to the C major scale. The entire 12-note pattern repeats so music can be played in higher and lower registers.

The white keys are called *natural* notes, spelled out as C♮, D♮, and so on. The black keys are *sharp* or *flat* notes, named by referring to the key/note to its left or right (below or above on the staff). For example, the note between C and D may be labeled C♯ or D♭.

Until we know which scale a note is associated with, we can't tell which name (sharp or flat) is the correct one for an accidental, so for now we'll use both. When writing notes on the staff, accidentals are placed **before** the note-head. When spelling or saying a note name, the accidental comes **after**.

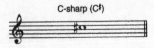

C-sharp (C♯)

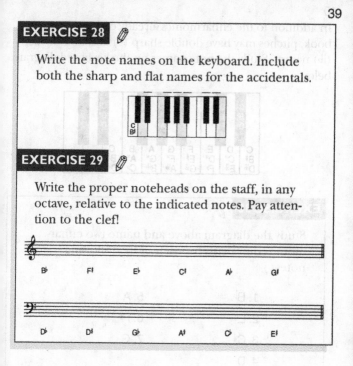

EXERCISE 28

Write the note names on the keyboard. Include both the sharp and flat names for the accidentals.

EXERCISE 29

Write the proper noteheads on the staff, in any octave, relative to the indicated notes. Pay attention to the clef!

B♭ F♯ E♭ C♯ A♭ G♯

D♭ D♯ G♭ A♯ C♯ E♯

Double Sharps and Flats

As you've noticed, it's possible for a pitch to have more than one name. These names are called *enharmonic equivalents.*

In addition to the enharmonics already covered in this book, pitches may have double sharp (✕) and double flat (♭♭) names. Study the note names on the keyboard diagram below.

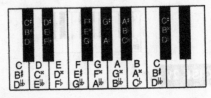

EXERCISE 30

Study the diagram above and name two enharmonic equivalents for each of the following notes.

1. B♭   5. A

2. E   6. F♯

3. C♯   7. G

4. D

Accidental Rules

An accidental applies to all notes of the same name that fall in the same measure, unless it is cancelled by another accidental. In the measure below, the first and second F notes are sharp. The third one is cancelled with a natural sign.

Accidentals are also cancelled by the bar line. Here, the F
in the second measure is natural.

Tied accidental notes may cross the bar line. However, the
accidental is cancelled when the tied note ends. Here, the
F♯ sustains across the bar line, but the next F, in measure
2, is natural.

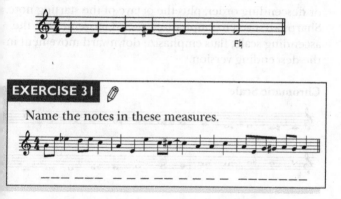

EXERCISE 31

Name the notes in these measures.

_____ _____ _ _____ _ _____

In common practice, *courtesy accidentals* are sometimes
used to remind the performer that an accidental has
been cancelled.

SCALES

A *scale* is a series of *ascending* (going up) or *descending* (going down) pitches. The starting note is called the root. The only repeated note is the ending root at the octave. In most of the scales we'll study, each letter of the alphabet is used only once.

The *chromatic scale* consists of only half steps. A complete chromatic scale is all twelve available pitches in ascending or descending order, plus the octave of the starting note. Sharps are used to emphasize upward movement in the ascending scale; flats emphasize downward movement in the descending version.

Chromatic Scale

The Major Scale

The major scale is the reference for other musical concepts, so we need to understand its construction well.

The *major scale formula* is this series of whole steps and half steps:

W–W–h–W–W–W–h

If we assign a number to each pitch (also called the *scale degrees*) in the major scale, we see that notes 3 and 4 are a half step apart. Notes 7 and 8 are also a half step apart. The other notes in the major scale are a whole step apart. When writing a scale numerically, half steps are marked with carets (^); whole steps are implied by the lack of a symbol.

1 2 3^4 5 6 7^8

Scale degree 1 is the root. The C major scale starts on C and follows the formula with these notes.

As previously mentioned, the naturally-occurring half steps (B–C and E–F) are the same as the half steps in the C major scale. This is one reason why we study C major first.

In order to maintain the formula for major scales that start from roots other than C, accidentals must be used. The way to find the correct accidentals is by remembering the natural half steps (B–C, E–F). Let's see this in action by building an F major scale.

There is already a naturally-occurring whole step from F to G, which fits the major scale formula, so no accidental is needed on G. Next, from G to A is a naturally-occurring whole step, also fitting the formula.

From A to B is a natural whole step, but the formula says we need a half step from 3 to 4 in the major scale. Therefore, B♭ is used instead of B, to reduce the whole step to a half step, and is the 4th degree of the F major scale.

Building an F Major Scale

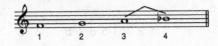

Identify the 4th degree of F major as B♭ and not as its enharmonic equivalent, A♯. Each scale degree number should get its own letter, and each letter is used exactly one time.

Continuing to examine the distances between successive notes, we find whole steps from B♭ to C, C to D, and D to E, and a natural half step from E to F. Play this scale to confirm that it has the familiar major-scale sound.

F Major Scale

When a scale starts on an accidental note, you may use either a sharp or flat to name it. The other note names should follow suit. Don't mix sharps and flats together in the same scale. One choice will have fewer accidentals than the other, except in the case of the G♭ and F♯ major scales (six flats or six sharps), making it easier to read. Always opt for ease of reading whenever possible.

EXERCISE 32 🖉

On a separate page of staff paper, use the formula to write major scales starting from each of these notes: C, G, D, A, E, B, F♯, and C♯; then from F, B♭, E♭, A♭, D♭, G♭, and C♭. Verify with your instrument. Which scales are enharmonic?

It's important to memorize the major scale formula (1 2 3^4 5 6 7^8) and practice spelling the major scale by starting from any note until it becomes easy. Along with the natural half steps (B–C, E–F), major scales are the foundation for most music theory. Likewise, being able to easily **sing** the major scale from any root is the foundation for all the subsequent ear-training exercises. Take your time—weeks or months, if needed—before moving on in this book.

EAR TRAINING DRILL 1

Using your instrument to find the roots, sing the major scales, ascending and descending, from each of the twelve possible starting notes in the order listed in the previous exercise. Count the scale degrees aloud as you sing each pitch: *"One, two, three, four, five, six, seven, eight. Eight, seven, six, five, four, three, two, one."*

The Natural Minor Scale

While there is only one major scale, there are several minor scales. The most important is called the *natural minor scale*. Memorize its formula and scale-degree spelling:

W h W W h W W
1 2 $^{\wedge \flat}$3 4 5 $^{\wedge \flat}$6 $\flat$7 8

The names $\flat$3, $\flat$6, and $\flat$7 are there to signify which notes are different when this scale is compared to the major scale. They do not always mean that the note gets a flat symbol when you spell the scale.

It turns out that when we start from the note A, the natural half steps (B–C, E–F) create a scale that fits the minor scale formula with no accidentals needed.

A Minor Scale

For minor scales other than A minor, accidentals must be used to follow the formula. Confirm that each note of this G minor scale fits the formula, with half steps from 2–3 and from 5–6.

G Minor Scale

EXERCISE 33 🖉

On a separate page of staff paper, write minor scales starting from each of these notes: A, D, G, C, F, B♭, E♭, and A♭; then from E, B, F♯, C♯, G♯, D♯, and A♯. Which scales are *enharmonic*?

EAR TRAINING DRILL 2

Using your instrument to provide the starting notes, sing natural minor scales, ascending and descending, from all twelve possible roots. As with major scales, sing the numbers, one through eight, and back.

Relative Minor and Major

The A minor scale shares the same arrangement of whole steps and half steps with C major, with a displacement of six steps. In other words, the white piano keys form a C major scale when starting from C, and they form an A minor scale when starting from A. The two scales are *relatives.*

C D E^F G A B^C   major scale
    A B^C D E^F G A   relative minor

This principle applies to scales from all roots. Each major scale has a relative minor. Repeat this slogan to help memorize how it works:

"The sixth degree of a major scale is the root of its relative minor."

We also need to know the principle in reverse. Each minor scale has a relative major, sharing its arrangement of whole and half steps, with a displacement of three steps.

A B^C D E^F G A   minor scale
C D E^F G A B^C   relative major

Chant this slogan to drive the point home:

"The third degree of a minor scale is the root of its relative major."

Notice that it can be faster to count down from eight than up from one to six to find the relative minor.

D E^F   F major scale
6 7 8
D E^F G A^B♭ C D   its relative, D minor

In practice, you'll want to know relative scales so well that you can name them without stopping to count.

EXERCISE 34 🖉

Name the relative minor scale for these
major scales.

1. A major	6. G major
2. F major	7. E♭ major
3. B♭ major	8. E major
4. D major	9. C major
5. F♯ major	10. B major

EXERCISE 35 🖉

Name the relative major scale for these
minor scales.

1. E minor	6. B minor
2. B♭ minor	7. G minor
3. D minor	8. G♯ minor
4. C♯ minor	9. C minor
5. F minor	10. A minor

INTERVALS

The payoff of learning intervals is a much better understanding of chords and melodies.

An *interval* (the distance between two pitches) may be measured from the lower note to the higher note (ascending) or from the higher note to the lower note (descending). Since the distance is the same either way, the name of the interval is the same whether it is ascending or descending.

Consecutive notes create a *melodic interval*. Simultaneous notes create a *harmonic interval*. Both are measured the same way. The interval name has two parts: *quantity* and *quality*, which must be used together to determine its exact size.

Interval Quantity

The quantity of an interval is expressed with a number. To find the quantity of an interval we count the lines and spaces from one pitch to the next in either direction. We can also use the letter names, assigning one number to each letter.

With the bottom note as 1, we count up to the higher note. Here is an ascending 5th.

We can also use the alphabet to find the quantity.

```
E F G A B
1 2 3 4 5
```

If the higher note is first, we have a descending 5th.

For speed, remember that in odd-numbered intervals (1, 3, 5, 7) both notes are on a line or on a space. In even-numbered intervals (2, 4, 6, 8) one note is on a line while the other is on a space. Notice there is no "zero" interval; notes of the same pitch are 1 (*unison* or *prime*).

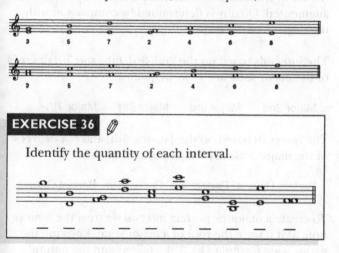

EXERCISE 36

Identify the quantity of each interval.

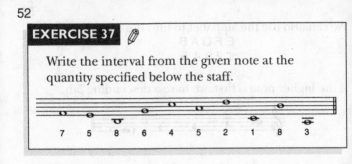

EXERCISE 37

Write the interval from the given note at the
quantity specified below the staff.

7   5   8   6   4   5   2   1   8   3

Interval Quality

Quality gives the exact size of an interval and is repre-
sented by a name: major, minor, perfect, diminished, or
augmented. Quality is determined by comparison with
the degrees of the major scale.

The intervals based on the 2nd, 3rd, 6th, and 7th degrees
of the major scale are *major* in quality:

Major 2nd   Major 3rd   Major 6th   Major 7th

The intervals based on the 1st, 4th, 5th, and 8th degrees
of the major scale are called *perfect* in quality:

Perfect Unison Perfect 4th Perfect 5th Perfect Octave

To create a major or perfect interval we treat the bottom
note as if it were the root of a major scale. Knowing the
major scale formula (1 2 3^4 5 6 7^8) and the natural
half steps (B–C, E–F) is essential here.

To create an **ascending major 3rd** starting from C, we
count up to the 3rd degree of the C major scale.

Ascending Major 3rd

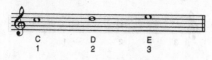

Let's do it again with a larger example. Below we find an **ascending major 6th** from B. Call B the root, then count up, following the major-scale formula.

Ascending Major 6th

Descending Intervals

To create a descending interval, we can count lines and spaces to roughly find the quantity. Then to get the correct accidental for the lower note, thus assuring the correct quality, we again use the major-scale formula, but this time counting backwards (8^7 6 5 4^3 2 1).

Let's create a **descending major 3rd** starting from C. Counting three lines and spaces shows the lower note will be an A of some kind. Now we count major-scale steps. From 3 to 2 is a whole step. If C is 3, then 2 must be B♭. Why? Because C–B is a natural half step.

From 2 to 1 of the major scale is also a whole step, so we find that 1 is A♭. (B♭ to A would only be a half step.)

Descending Major 3rd

Here's a larger example, a descending major 6th from B♭. Counting lines and spaces we find a D of some kind, but this is only the quantity. By following the major-scale formula, making sure there are whole steps between all degrees, except for a half step from 4 down to 3, we find that 1 is D♭.

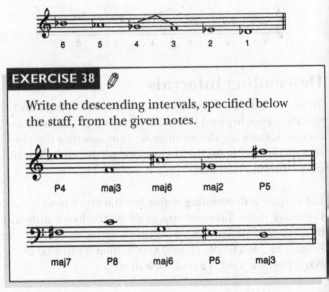

EXERCISE 38

Write the descending intervals, specified below the staff, from the given notes.

Minor, Diminished, and Augmented Intervals

Diminution (the act of diminishing) is the **reduction** in quality of an interval. (Remember that quality is the exact interval size.) The opposite, *augmentation*, is the **increase** in the quality of an interval. With diminution or augmentation, we change the accidentals on the notes. The basic quantity (numeric value and letter names) of the interval stays the same.

When a major interval (2, 3, 6, 7) is reduced by a half step, it becomes *minor*. This smaller interval could be created by **lowering the top note** or by **raising the bottom note**.

Diminution of Major 3rd to Minor 3rd

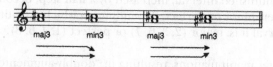

If this interval undergoes diminution by another half step, it becomes *diminished*.

Diminution of Minor 3rd to Diminished 3rd

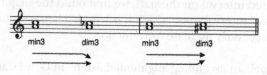

When a perfect interval (1, 4, 5, 8) undergoes diminution by a half step, it immediately becomes *diminished* in quality. There is no minor level for intervals 1, 4, 5, or 8.

How Interval Qualities Change

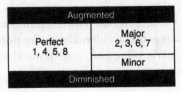

Both major and perfect intervals become *augmented* in quality when augmented by a half step. A minor interval becomes major, then augmented in quality by going up two half steps.

A diminished interval, increased by a half step, becomes either minor or perfect, depending on which quantity of interval it is: major (2, 3, 6, 7) or perfect (1, 4, 5, 8).

Larger manipulations, resulting in "doubly-augmented" or "doubly-diminished" intervals are also possible but are rarely needed.

To construct or identify a minor, diminished, or augmented interval on the staff, we first build the major or perfect interval upon which it is based. Then we make the necessary increase or reduction.

To spell an **ascending augmented 5th** from G, we start with a perfect 5th from the G major scale. Augment by one half step. G to D♯ is an augmented 5th.

Ascending Augmented 5th from G

To spell an **ascending minor 7th** from C♯, we find the 7th of the C♯ major scale, then diminish (reduce) by one half step. B is the minor 7th of C♯.

Ascending Minor 7th from C♯

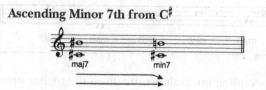

Let's stay with C♯ and, this time, find the **ascending diminished 7th**. Again, use the C♯ major scale, counting up to the major 7th, but this time diminish by two half steps. An ascending diminished 7th from C♯ is B♭.

Ascending Diminished 7th from C♯

EXERCISE 39 ✏

Write the specified interval above the provided note.

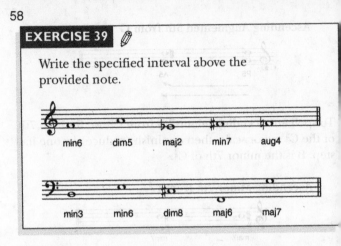

min6   dim5   maj2   min7   aug4

min3   min6   dim8   maj6   maj7

For descending intervals, we are given the higher note. We find the perfect or major descending interval first, counting down the major scale. Then we move the lower note to fit the exact quality we need.

If a minor or diminished interval is desired, we raise the lower note, moving it closer to the higher note, thus reducing the size of the interval.

Descending Diminished 5th from B

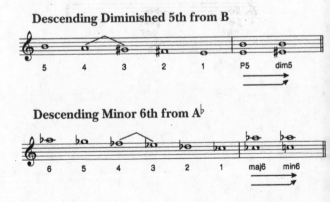

5   4   3   2   1   P5   dim5

Descending Minor 6th from A♭

6   5   4   3   2   1   maj6   min6

If an augmented interval is desired, we drop the lower note farther away from the higher one, increasing the interval.

Descending Augmented 2nd from A

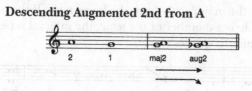

Descending Augmented 4th from F#

EXERCISE 40 🖉

Write the specified interval below the provided note.

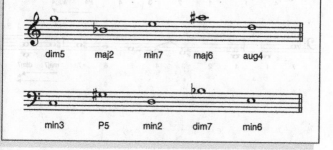

After constructing these intervals, we also need to make sure we can identify them. In this case, we can start from the lower note and avoid any backward counting.

Start with the major scale from the lower note. If the higher note is a member of the scale, the interval is perfect or major in quality.

If the higher note is **not** a member of the lower note's major scale, then count how many half steps away the note is from the scale member with the same letter name. If it is higher, the interval is augmented. If it is lower, the interval is minor or diminished.

EXERCISE 41

Write the names of these intervals, specifying the quality and quantity.

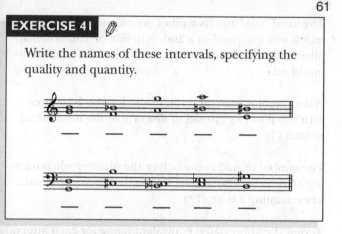

EAR TRAINING DRILL 3

Play and then immediately sing each of the twelve unique intervals, from a minor 2nd to an octave, from the root C. Change to the key of G and sing the intervals again.

Abbreviating Interval Names

A perfect or major interval is implied by not stating the quality. For example, a 2nd is always a major 2nd unless you say it is minor, augmented, or diminished. The same applies to 3rds, 6ths, and 7ths. A unison, 4th, 5th, or octave interval is always perfect unless it is called something else.

The word "sharp" and its symbol (♯) is used to mean augmented. For instance, a ♯5 is an augmented 5th.

The word "flat" and its symbol (♭) are used to mean minor when applied to a 2nd, 3rd, 6th, or 7th. When applied to a perfect interval (1, 4, 5, or 8), "flat" means diminished.

When a major interval is diminished, it can be written with two flats (♭♭) instead of *dim* or *d* or the diminished symbol (°).

The symbol should come before the number when naming an interval (♭3). Again, the symbol comes afterward when naming a note (E♭).

Review the abbreviated equivalent name for each interval aloud: ♭3 = minor 3rd, ♭5 = diminished 5th, etc.

Interval Mnemonics
You may find interval recognition easier when you can compare what you are singing to a familiar melody. Here are some traditional references to help remember interval sounds. It only works if you can really sing the little melodies, so you might need to practice that at first.

Notice that the first note of a melody is not always the tonic note! For instance, in "Happy Birthday," the major 2nd interval is from the 5th to the 6th in the major scale.

Minor 2nd	"Jaws" (movie theme)
Major 2nd	"Happy Birthday to You"
Minor 3rd	"Greensleeves"
Major 3rd	"Oh, When the Saints Go Marching In"
Perfect 4th	"Here Comes the Bride"
Diminished 5th	"The Simpsons"
Perfect 5th	"Twinkle, Twinkle, Little Star"
Minor 6th	"The Entertainer" (3rd and 4th notes)
Major 6th	"My Bonnie Lies over the Ocean"
Minor 7th	"Star Trek" (original TV closing theme)
Major 7th	"Superman" (movie theme)
Octave	"Somewhere over the Rainbow"

f these songs are unfamiliar to you, find and learn them
s part of your music education. Also listen for the inter-
als in other songs you know.

Make interval recognition part of your daily practice. It's
he foundation for transcription of melodies and chord
rogressions.

EXERCISE 42

Write down 100 random intervals, naming them
and writing them on the staff. Then record them
with an instrument, mixing both melodic and
harmonic intervals, if possible. Verbally an-
nounce the number of each example (1–100) on
the recording. Then go back and transcribe
them, and check your results against your key.

Compound Intervals

Compound intervals are larger than an octave. They can be considered equivalent to their counterparts an octave lower, which are called *simple* intervals. The 9th interval, for instance, is a compound 2nd (a 2nd plus an octave) and is likewise major in quality.

Compound and Equivalent Simple Intervals

	Major		Perfect
9th	2nd + octave		
10th	3rd + octave		
		11th	4th + octave
		12th	5th + octave
13th	6th + octave		
14th	7th + octave		
		15th	two octaves

EXERCISE 43

Write the name of each compound interval.

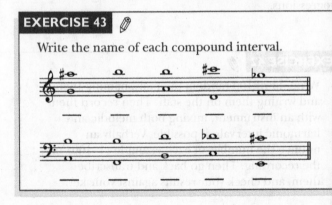

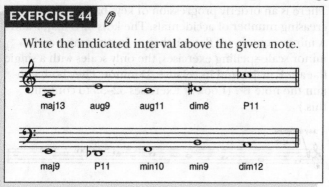

EXERCISE 44

Write the indicated interval above the given note.

maj13   aug9   aug11   dim8   P11

maj9   P11   min10   min9   dim12

Key Signatures

Now that you have an understanding of intervals, let's revisit scales.

At any given time, only one scale dominates a piece of music, so it's easier to write and read if we specify its accidentals at the beginning of the song or section. This is a *key signature*, and we say that we are in a *key* based on that scale.

> The sensation produced by a key is called *tonality*. It's the feeling that one particular note is the most stable and likely place for musical phrases to end. This note, the root of the scale, is called the *tonic* of the key.

Most students need several weeks of study to understand and apply key signatures at first. Be patient and take frequent breaks.

There is an orderly progression of keys based on the increasing number of accidentals. The keys of C major and A minor contain no flats or sharps. In our major and minor scale-spelling exercises, the only scales with a single flat are F major and its relative, D minor. They both contain the note B♭. (Look at Exercises 32–33 to confirm this.)

The only scales with **two** flats are B♭ major and its relative, G minor. They contain the same flat as before, B♭, and another one, E♭.

The only scales with **three** flats are E♭ major and C minor. They use the same flats as before, plus A♭.

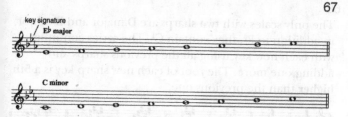

Each successive flat key signature contains all the flats previously used, plus one more. The root of each new **flat** key is a **4th higher** than the previous one. The flats should always be written in the same symmetrical pattern in treble and bass clef. Memorize and always list the flats in this order: B♭, E♭, A♭, D♭, G♭, C♭, F♭.

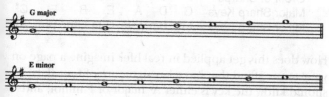

After more than six flats (G♭ major or E♭ minor keys and beyond) we start creating keys that are pretty hard to spell. At this point they are enharmonic to **sharp** keys that use fewer accidentals. For instance, C♭ major with seven flats is enharmonic to B major, which we'll soon see has just five sharps, making B major a little easier to use.

The only scales with **one** sharp are G major and E minor. They both contain F♯.

The only scales with **two** sharps are D major and B minor; in addition to F♯, they contain C♯. The series continues with each new key using all the previous sharps and adding one more. The root of each new sharp key is a **5th higher** than the previous one.

Note that sharps don't follow a perfectly symmetrical pattern on the staff as flats did. Rather than use ledger lines, the sharps on A and B are written an octave lower on both bass and treble clef.

It's best to memorize all of the key signatures, to instantly know which possible (major or minor) key you are working with as soon as you see it.

	1	2	3	4	5	6	7
Order of Flats	B♭	E♭	A♭	D♭	G♭	C♭	F♭
Major Flat Keys	F	B♭	E♭	A♭	D♭	G♭	C♭
Minor Flat Keys	Dm	Gm	Cm	Fm	B♭m	E♭m	A♭m

	1	2	3	4	5	6	7
Order of Sharps	F♯	C♯	G♯	D♯	A♯	E♯	B♯
Major Sharp Keys	G	D	A	E	B	F♯	C♯
Minor Sharp Keys	Em	Bm	F♯m	C♯m	G♯m	D♯m	A♯m

How does this get applied in real life? Imagine a page on your music stand that has a key signature of four flats. You should know the key is either A♭ major or F minor, and that the four flat notes in these keys are B♭, E♭, A♭, and D♭.

Circle of 5ths

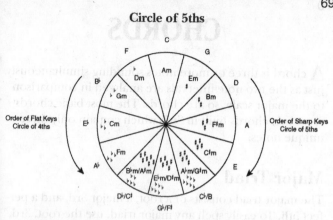

Order of Flat Keys
Circle of 4ths

Order of Sharp Keys
Circle of 5ths

EXERCISE 45 ✐

Get 30 index cards and draw a staff, a clef, and a
key signature on the blank side of each, making
separate cards for treble and bass clef. Copy each
signature's exact arrangement from the grand
staff examples given on page 65. On the other
side, write the name of the keys (major and
minor) and the order of the accidentals.

Use the cards frequently to drill your knowledge of key
signatures, for a few minutes at a time, until you are com-
fortable and accurate with it.

CHORDS

A chord is three or more notes sounding simultaneously. Just as the two-note intervals are analyzed in comparison to the major scale, so are chords. The most basic chords are *triads*: chords built in 3rds which contain only three unique notes.

Major Triad

The major triad consists of a root, a major 3rd, and a perfect 5th. To easily spell any major triad, use the root, 3rd, and 5th of the major scale. The major triad is implied by a chord name with no mention of quality.

EXERCISE 46

Write major triads from these starting notes. Use the major-scale formula.

Minor Triad

The minor triad consists of a root, a minor 3rd, and a perfect 5th. There is more than one way to spell a minor triad. First, spell a major scale and extract the root, 3rd, and 5th. Diminish the 3rd by a half step to make the triad minor.

Another method is to take the root, ♭3, and 5th from a natural minor scale with the same root as the desired minor triad.

EXERCISE 47

Write minor triads from these starting notes.

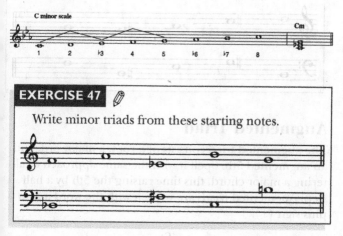

Diminished Triad

The diminished triad consists of a root, a minor 3rd, and a diminished 5th. We'll spell it with the major-chord-altering approach, this time diminishing the 3rd and the 5th by a half step. Diminished chords are written with the word *dim* or a small circle (°).

EXERCISE 48

Write diminished triads from these starting notes.

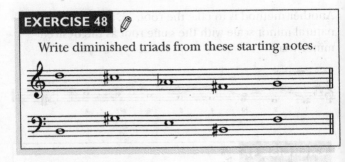

Augmented Triad

The augmented triad consists of a root, a major 3rd, and an augmented 5th. Spell it with the same approach of altering a major chord, this time raising the 5th by a half step. Augmented triads are written with the word *aug* or a plus sign (+).

EXERCISE 49

Write augmented triads from these starting notes.

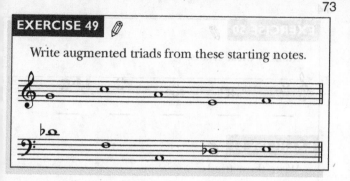

Suspended Triad

Though technically not a true triad because it's not built in 3rds, this three-note chord is important to know because it appears quite frequently. The sus4 chord contains a root, a perfect 4th, and a perfect 5th. If a chord has only the word *sus*, with no number after it, you may assume it is a sus4 chord.

Another popular chord is the sus2, consisting of a root, major 2nd, and a perfect 5th.

74

EXERCISE 50

Identify these triads.

___ ___ ___ ___ ___

EXERCISE 51

Write these triads.

Esus4   Absus2   D#sus4   G#sus4   C#sus2

Gsus4   Dbsus2   Asus4   Fsus2   Bsus4

Voicing and Inversion

The particular arrangement of notes in a chord is called its *voicing*. The notes may be *voiced* in any order, spread out, or doubled in different octaves without changing the identity of the chord.

When the root of a chord is its lowest note, the chord is said to be in *root position*.

If the 3rd is the lowest note, the chord is said to be in *first inversion*. To specify the inversion, you can follow the chord name with a slash and the bass (lowest) note.

If the 5th is in the lowest position, the chord is in *second inversion*.

EXERCISE 52

Identify and write the chord names, with the bass notes to the right of the slashes. Then name the inversions.

76

Write the chords on the staff in the specified inversion.

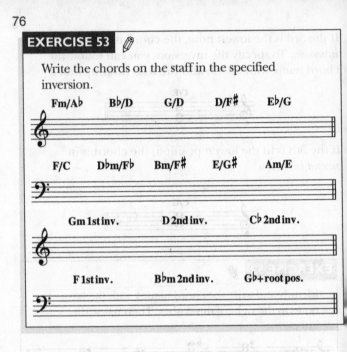

| Fm/Ab | Bb/D | G/D | D/F# | Eb/G |

| F/C | Dbm/Fb | Bm/F# | E/G# | Am/E |

| Gm 1st inv. | D 2nd inv. | Cb 2nd inv. |

| F 1st inv. | Bbm 2nd inv. | Gb+ root pos. |

Arpeggiation

An *arpeggio* is the notes of a chord played in sequence, rather than simultaneously. If your instrument is *monophonic* (capable of producing only one note at a time) *arpeggiation* is the only way for you to express chordal, or *harmonic*, information.

An arpeggio may start and finish on any chord tone and on any beat of the music. Learning to identify groups of notes as arpeggiated chord members makes many jobs easier: reading, memorizing, improvising. A root-position arpeggio (or chord) contains notes on all lines or all spaces only. When chords and arpeggios are inverted (or spread out across octaves), they can be harder to recognize on the staff. In many cases, any sequence of notes that doesn't move in a scalar fashion (line, space, line, space, etc.) is likely to be an arpeggio.

EXERCISE 54

Circle and label the arpeggios in this example.

EXERCISE 55

Play triads in root position with the qualities we've studied—major, minor, diminished, augmented, sus4, and sus2—from all twelve possible roots. As you play, **sing** the triads as root-position arpeggios. Practice this assignment a few minutes at a time for several weeks.

Notice the general emotional quality of each triad type. A major triad sounds happy, while a minor triad sounds sad by comparison. The diminished triad can be thought of as ambiguous and kind of scary, while the augmented triad sounds tense and expectant. The sus4 triad sounds like it should resolve to a major triad on the same root, like the "amen" at the end of a hymn.

MORE RHYTHMS AND METERS

Tempo

Tempo (Italian for *time*) is the speed of the music. Tempo may be indicated as a number of beats per minute (abbreviated *bpm*) written over the music. The note that equals the beat is specified. In this 4/4 example, quarter notes are the basic unit. A tempo change from 60 to 100 is specified.

Italian terms are also used to indicate tempo, especially in classical music. These terms predate the invention of the metronome, so there is overlap and variation between what is intended by different composers.

Largo	Slow, broad	40–60
Larghetto	Somewhat slow	60–70
Adagio	Slow	60–80
Andante	Walking, steady	60–100
Moderato	Moderate	70–120
Allegro	Happy, lively	90–160
Presto	Fast	160–200
Prestissimo	Very fast	200–

In addition to tempo-setting terms, we should also be familiar with these basic tempo-changing terms that may be written over the music.

Accelerando	Speeding up
Ritardando	Slowing down
A Tempo	At the original tempo
Rubato	At the same general tempo, but with free rhythmic interpretation.

Sixteenth Notes

By dividing a quarter-note beat into four equal parts, we get four *sixteenth notes* or *sixteenth rests.* An eighth note is equal in duration to two sixteenth notes, or to two sixteenth rests.

We can add sixteenths to the bottom of our pyramid of durations. Two sixteenths equal one eighth. Four sixteenths equal one quarter, and so on.

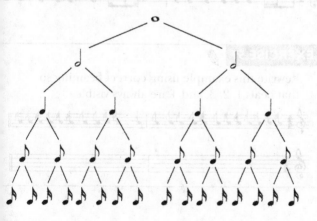

The sixteenth notes between numbered beats are counted as "e-and-a". There are sixteen sixteenth notes in a measure of 4/4 time. They are beamed so that beats are easy to see in the measure.

EXERCISE 56

Practice counting sixteenth notes aloud with a metronome. As always, continue to tap your foot in quarter notes.

Beams also connect eighth notes and sixteenth notes within the same beat.

EXERCISE 57

Rewrite this example using correct beaming so that beats 1, 2, 3, and 4 are always visible.

Triplet Rhythms

Triplets are produced by dividing the beat into three equal parts. Writing the number 3 at the stem end tells the player to evenly space three notes in the time normally occupied by two notes of the written value. For example, an *eighth-note triplet* is equal in duration to two eighth notes. Count the triplet with "one-and-a, two-and-a," etc. Tap your foot in quarter notes while you count and clap your hands on each divided beat.

The triplet figure with the middle note removed is called a *shuffle.* As before, it's important to keep the foot tapping in quarter notes. Continue counting "one-and-a" while clapping only the first and third notes.

Cut Time

In 4/4, or common time, the beat is equal to a quarter note. When 4/4 time is played at a high *tempo* (speed), it becomes difficult to count and tap the foot. In this case we can count two half notes per measure, tapping the foot at half the original tempo. The notation in each measure stays the same, but now the time signature is 2/2. This is also called *cut time*, sometimes indicated by a C with a vertical slash (¢).

3/4 Time

3/4 time has three quarter notes per measure. A song using this meter is often called a *waltz*. 3/4 is used in all styles of music, especially classical, folk, and country.

When a song in 3/4 time is played at a high tempo, it becomes difficult to count and tap the foot for each beat. In this case, the time signature stays the same, but we tap the foot only once per measure. This is called taking the measures "in one."

Straight and Shuffle Feels

The *feel* of a piece of music refers to how the basic pulse is divided. In all cases, we only tap our feet on the pulses. Once we're tapping our feet steadily on the pulses, we can change the way we count the smaller divisions to get the feel.

In a *straight* feel, beats are divided evenly in two. For 4/4 or 3/4 time, this means that all eighth notes are of the same duration. Straight feels are commonly used in rock, funk, Latin, and many other grooves.

In a *shuffle* feel, the beats are divided into **three** equal parts. The second part of each beat is not attacked—just the first and third.

"1 & a 2 & a 3 & a 4 & a"

We can feel this as a repeating pattern of long and short notes. Over the music we write that two eighth notes are equal to the triplet-based shuffle rhythm. Count the long and short notes as "1 a 2 a 3 a 4 a."

HARMONY

Harmony is the study of chords and how they work together. Though it has many branches (classical, blues, jazz, modal, etc.), we'll focus on diatonic harmony, as it creates the standard for describing and comparing all other harmonic concepts. These are not rules to be followed but rather principles for understanding what we hear and describing what we write.

Harmonized Scales

Major

When studying key signatures, we learned that at any given time a song is dominated by a single scale that creates a key. Strictly speaking, a key contains seven chords that only use scale notes, called *diatonic chords*. To spell these chords, we begin by writing the 3rd and 5th scale notes over the tonic. The first chord in the key of C is a C major triad built from the C major scale.

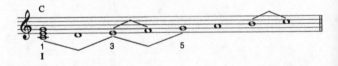

Because these diatonic triads are built in the same fashion in any key, we may label them by the number of the scale degree they are built from. Traditionally, Roman numerals are used to distinguish chords from the many other things we use Arabic numerals for. We can say that the tonic chord, a C major triad in our first example, is the *I ("one") chord* in the key of C.

In this book, as in many other theory books, uppercase Roman numerals (I, IV, V, etc.) are used to imply major chords. Lowercase Roman numerals (ii, iii, vi) are used to imply minor chords. This allows the qualities (*major* or *minor*) or their abbreviations (*maj* for *major*, *m* for *minor*) to be left off the names of triads. For diminished chords, the little circle will be added to lowercase numerals (e.g., vii°).

Some books use differing methods; for instance, some use only uppercase letters for all chords and always specify the quality. There is no rigid standard, but as long as everyone involved with your music agrees on the method, any system for notating chords with numbers is fine.

To build the *ii* (*"two"*) *chord*, we again use alternating notes from the scale. This time we use degrees 2, 4, and 6. The major scale formula (W–W–h–W–W–W–h or 1 2 3^4 5 6 7^8) creates an interval of a minor 3rd from steps 2 to 4 in the scale. From 4 to 6 is a major 3rd. The result of these two intervals is a minor triad built on step 2 of the scale. In the key of C, the ii chord is Dm.

Continuing the process of building chords from alternating scale notes, the *iii chord* from degrees 3, 5, and 7 gives us another minor triad. In C, this chord is Em.

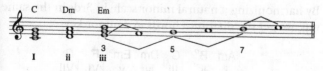

Moving on, we get major triads on steps 4 and 5, another minor triad on step 6, and, finally, a diminished triad on step 7. The diminished triad has two minor 3rds in a row: from 7 to 9 and 9 to 11 in the major scale.

Memorize the order of triad qualities in a major key. Major–minor–minor–Major–Major–minor–diminished:

$$I–ii–iii–IV–V–vi–vii°$$

EXERCISE 58

Write the diatonic triads in all twelve major keys on staff paper. Using a key signature for each, write the chord names above the staff and the Roman numeral (also called the *function*) below. Play all of the triads as chords, arpeggiate, and sing as arpeggios. To get you started, here are the triads in the key of G.

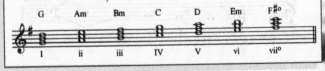

Minor

By harmonizing a natural minor scale in 3rds in the same way, we get the diatonic chords in a minor key.

Am	B°	C	Dm	Em	F	G
i	ii°	♭III	iv	v	♭VI	♭VII

Following the principle of relative-minor and major scales, the diatonic chords in a minor key are the same as the chords in major, only starting from the 6th.

C Dm Em^F G Am B°^C   -major

        Am B°^C D Em^F G Am   -relative minor

EXERCISE 59 🖉

Write the diatonic triads in all twelve minor keys on staff paper. Using a key signature for each, write the chord names above the staff and the Roman numeral below. Play all of the triads as chords, arpeggiate, and sing as arpeggios. To get you started, here are the triads in the key of Em.

Harmonic Minor

Although the diatonic v chord in a minor key is a minor triad, a major triad is often used instead for a stronger resolution to the i chord. The raised 3rd of this chord is a major 7th (or *leading tone*) of the overall key. This note imparts more tension toward the tonic than the ♭7th. Substituting the leading tone for the minor 7th changes the natural minor scale to a *harmonic minor scale*.

A Harmonic Minor Scale
A   B   C   D   E   F   G♯   A
1   2^♭3   4   5^♭6 – 7^   8

Along with the major V triad (E–G#–B), harmonizing the harmonic minor scale also yields an augmented triad on ♭III (C–E–G#) and a diminished triad from the leading tone (vii°, G#–B–D).

The ♭III+ chord is seldom used, but the other new chords on V and vii are very common. Compare the original diatonic triads in A minor to those with the new V and vii° chords.

Am B° C Dm E F G#°
i ii° ♭III iv V ♭VI vii°

EXERCISE 60 🖉

Using the necessary accidentals, add the V and vii° chords derived from harmonic minor after the harmonized minor scales you wrote in the previous exercise (**EXERCISE 59**). Name the chords above and write the Roman numerals below.

Major Harmony in Diatonic Seventh Chords

Seventh chords are four-note chords, the next step up from triads.

The diatonic seventh chords in a major key can be built by stacking 3rds just as we built the diatonic triads. Here they are in the key of C.

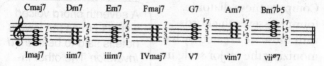

The I and IV chords produced by the scale are *major seventh chords*, spelled 1–3–5–7 from their respective roots.

> A note name followed only by the number 7 (or higher)—without the words *maj* or *m*—always signifies a dominant chord (one with a major 3rd and a minor 7th).

The ii, iii, and vi chords produced by the scale are *minor seventh chords*, spelled 1–♭3–5–♭7 from their respective roots.

For the V, the scale produces an important chord type we have not seen yet, the *dominant seventh chord*. From its root, this chord is spelled 1–3–5–♭7.

The vii chord produced by the scale is called a *minor seventh flat five chord*. From its root, this chord is spelled 1–♭3–♭5–♭7. Another name for this chord is *half-diminished*.

The addition of sevenths to the diatonic chords does not change their function within the key, but adds tension (referred to as *dissonance* in this situation) and a sense of sophistication. This does not mean that seventh chords are better or that they should be used more frequently. The decision of which type of chord to use is based on how the chords support the melody and the desired stylistic or emotional effect.

Compare these diatonic, four-note seventh chords with those we created by harmonizing the major scale in triads. Though they're based on the same triads, the names of the chords on degrees V and vii are quite different. The V triad is major (1–3–5); the V7 chord is dominant (1–3–5–♭7).

> A seventh chord voiced with its 7th as the lowest note is said to be in *third inversion*. The other inversion principles we've studied also apply to seventh chords.

The question of why the diatonic vii° triad is diminished (1–♭3–♭5), while the corresponding seventh chord is often called "half-diminished" merits some review of interval qualities in the Intervals chapter.

Staying in the key of C, on step vii we have a chord with these notes: B–D–F–A. We already know the first three notes form a diminished triad. Looking at the 7th interval, from B to A, recall that we measure an interval by creating a major scale from the lower note. The B major scale contains A♯ on its (major) seventh degree. Lowering it one half step to A converts the 7th to the minor quality. The complete chord is a diminished triad with a minor 7th. The 7th itself is not diminished!

The Diminished Seventh Chord

Only lowering the 7th another half step would change it to a diminished interval. The new chord containing a diminished triad with a diminished 7th gets the "fully-diminished" name.

Bdim7 or B°7 = B–D–F–A♭ (1–♭3–♭5–♯♯7)

The diminished seventh chord is often described as sounding tense yet uncertain; it wants to move but it's unclear which chord should follow it. Uncertainty is a source of fear, so this chord is often used at scary moments in movie soundtracks.

The m7♭5, or half-diminished, seventh chord is sometimes labeled with the same small circle, but with a slash through it: Bm7♭5 = Bⱷ7.

EXERCISE 61 🖉

On the staff, write the indicated chords.

Am7♭5   G°7   F♯m7♭5   B°7   C♯°7

Bm7♭5   D°7   F°7   E♭m7♭5   B♭°7

EXERCISE 62 🖉

Add sevenths to the diatonic triads, major and minor, that you previously wrote out on the staff. Do this in all twelve major and twelve minor keys, labeling each chord with its name and function. Then play, listen, and sing the notes, and verbally describe the sensation you get from each chord quality.

Minor Harmony in Diatonic Seventh Chords

By extending the chords of the harmonized minor scale to sevenths, we get the same chords as those in its relative major key. We also add the harmony created by the harmonic minor scale, with its raised seventh degree.

Strictly Diatonic Minor

Am7	Bm7♭5	Cmaj7	Dm7	Em7	Fmaj7	G7
im7	iim7♭5	♭IIImaj7	ivm7	vm7	♭VImaj7	♭VII7

Minor With Commonly-Used Harmonic-Minor Variations

Am7	Bm7♭5	Cmaj7	Dm7	E7	Fmaj7	G♯°7
im7	iim7♭5	♭IIImaj7	ivm7	V7	♭VImaj7	vii°7

In common practice, minor keys often contain a mixture of chords derived from both natural-minor and harmonic-minor scales. A typical song in a minor key may contain either (or both) the vm7 and V7 chords. It may also contain either (or both) the ♭VII7 and vii°7. This also applies to triadic minor progressions—they may contain either the v or V and either the ♭VII or vii°.

EXERCISE 63 ✎

Write the V7 and vii°7 chords for the harmonized minor scales in **EXERCISE 62**.

HARMONIC ANALYSIS

Harmonic analysis means finding the key center for a chord progression, based on the major and minor scale harmony we have learned. We also give each chord a Roman numeral that shows how it relates to the tonic chord. The key center and the chord functions tell us which scale(s) may be used to create a melody. Being able to identify keys, chord functions, and the corresponding scales is essential for composers and improvisers. For all examples, as in real life, it's also important to listen to the chords working together and find the key center by singing the tonic note. With that in mind, make sure that you play and listen to all the examples in this chapter on a chordal instrument like piano or guitar. If that's not possible, arpeggiate the progressions on your instrument.

Major Key Centers

To find a key center, we try to fit the chords of a song section into a harmonized major scale, remembering its two most important aspects:

1) The major scale formula, with half steps from 3 to 4 and from 7 to 8. This gives the distance from chord root to chord root in a major key.

$$1 \ 2 \ 3^4 \ 5 \ 6 \ 7^8$$
$$W \ W \ h \ W \ W \ W \ h$$

2) The qualities of the chords produced by harmonizing the scale.

Imaj7 iim7 iiim7 IVmaj7 V7 vim7 viim7♭5

We try to fit as many chords as possible into one key. Many songs do not change keys at all. Let's start with a very short sample progression.

$$E^\flat maj7 \mid Dm7 \mid F7 \mid$$

Because it's a major seventh chord, $E^\flat maj7$ may be I, or it may be IV. These are the only two places in the harmonized major scale where this chord type occurs. If the chord is the I, then we are in the key of $E^\flat$ major.

On the other hand, if $E^\flat maj7$ is the IV chord, then we must count down the major scale formula, using the correct whole and half steps to find the tonic. Start on the right and follow the arrows, step by step, making sure the major scale formula is followed.

$$B^\flat \leftarrow C \leftarrow D \leftarrow E^\flat$$
$$I \quad ii \quad iii \, ^\wedge IV$$

The first chord of the progression, then, says we are in either the key of $E^\flat$ or $B^\flat$.

Look at the next chord of the progression. Dm7 may be ii, iii, or vi. By counting down major scales with D on each of these steps, we find that its possible keys are C, $B^\flat$, or F. At this point we notice that the first two chords, $E^\flat maj7$ and Dm7, are only common to the key of $B^\flat$. The progression can be analyzed as **IV–iii** in the key of $B^\flat$.

Moving on to F7 (all chords must be analyzed because we never know when the key might change), we realize that the diatonic harmony we know only includes dominant chords in one place: the V. Counting down the major scale formula from V to I, we see that F7 is the V in the

ey of B♭. The entire progression is in the key of B♭, and
he B♭ major scale may be used for melody and improvisa-
ion over all three chords.

For the harmonic analysis, we write the key center below,
ollowed by a colon and the chord functions.

	E♭maj7	Dm7	F7	
B♭:	IVmaj7	iiim7	V7

EXERCISE 64

Analyze these short progressions and tell which
major key (or keys) they might be in, providing
Roman numerals for each. If there are two possible keys, put the second analysis on a new line.
Note: For any dominant seventh or m7♭5 chord,
only one major key is possible (until we intro-
duce non-diatonic chords), so you can save time
by analyzing it first, but always analyze all the
chords. Don't worry about minor keys for now.

1. Fmaj7–Dm7–C7   6. F♯m7♭5

2. C♯m7–F♯m7   7. Em7–F♯m7–A7

3. Am7–Cmaj7–Em7   8. G♯m7–C♯m7–Emaj7

4. B♭m7–Fm7–A♭7   9. Fm7–B♭7

5. Fmaj7–Cmaj7   10. A♭maj7–Cm7–D♭maj7

Triad progressions are analyzed using the same method as seventh-chord progressions, but they can be a little more ambiguous because the I, IV, and V chords are all of the same quality: major. It may be necessary to use your ear to help identify the I chord. In many songs, the first or the last chord of a section such as the chorus or verse is the I chord. It's a good place to start.

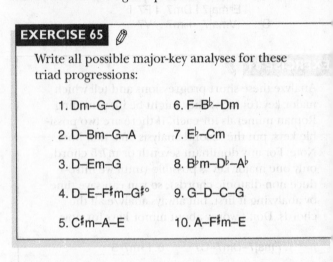

EXERCISE 65

Write all possible major-key analyses for these triad progressions:

1. Dm–G–C

2. D–Bm–G–A

3. D–Em–G

4. D–E–F#m–G#°

5. C#m–A–E

6. F–B♭–Dm

7. E♭–Cm

8. B♭m–D♭–A♭

9. G–D–C–G

10. A–F#m–E

Non-Diatonic Chords

Very often we'll find one or more chords in a progression that don't fit the harmonized scale, followed by chords in the same key as before. There are various principles musicians use to categorize these non-diatonic chords in advanced harmonic analysis. However, for now, when one appears, we'll simply label it by its distance from the tonic chord and its given quality, not considering it a key change.

```
      A  D  Dm A
A:    I  IV iv  I

      E  G   A  B
E:    I ♭III IV V

      Cmaj7 Am7 G7 Fmaj7  B♭7  Cmaj7
C:    Imaj7 vim7 V7 IVmaj7 ♭VII7 Imaj7

      F  G7  B♭ F
F:    I  II7 IV I
```

Minor Key Centers

The same general method of using a harmonized scale is used for identifying and analyzing minor-key progressions. The chords that come from the harmonic minor scale are important exceptions to watch for. Although these also are considered diatonic, when improvising or composing melodies over these chords, the scale switches from natural minor to harmonic minor and back again.

> In practice, the m7♭5 chord is usually the ii chord in a minor key center; the use of viim7♭5 chords in major keys is not so common. A dominant seventh chord is likely to be V7 or ♭VII7 in either a major or a minor key. Look for the I- or i-chord resolution immediately following it.

```
      Em  Cmaj7    Am7  F#m7♭5 B7  Em
Em:   i  ♭VImaj7  ivm7 iim7♭5  V7   i

      Eb  Dm  D7  Gm7
Gm:  ♭VI  v   V7  im7
```

EXERCISE 66

For each progression, write the minor key and chord functions.

1. Dm7♭5–G7–Cm7–Fm7

2. Em–D7–Am–B7

3. Fm7–E♭7–D♭maj7–C7

4. Em–Bm–Am

5. Gm–B♭–Cm–D7

6. Am7–Dm7–Bm7♭5–E7

7. F–C7–B♭maj7–Dm

8. B♭m–A♭–D♭–F7

9. Cm–Gm–E♭–A♭

10. F#m–E–A–C#7

Stock Progressions

Stock chord progressions are ones that appear in numerous songs. Learn to recognize them in any key; it will speed up your ability to find the correct scale to play over the progression. The most important chord combination to recognize is V–I in major or V–i in minor. These two chords alone are enough to establish a tonality.

I–IV–V–I
iim7–V7–Imaj7
iii–vi–ii–V–I
I–vi–iim–V
I–IV–♭VII–I
vi–IV–I–V

EXERCISE 67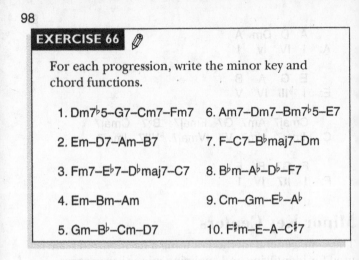

Write out the above progressions in the keys of F, B♭, E♭, A♭, D♭, G♭, B, E, A, D, G, and C.

Modulation

A *modulation* is a change of key. On the staff, a new key signature may be used, but usually only if the new key lasts for a long time. In any harmonic analysis, the new key is followed by a colon, followed by the chord functions.

Direct modulation occurs when the first chord in the new key is not a member of the previous key. The effect is abrupt and fairly obvious: The old I chord or tonic note is replaced with a new one in the listener's ear.

	C	F	G	C		A	E	C#m	D
C:	I	IV	V	I	A:	I	V	iii	IV

Pivot chord modulation is when the new key starts with chord(s) that are shared with the old key. The effect is more subtle. The listener may not notice the key change for several measures, if at all. In the harmonic analysis, the pivot chord(s) are labeled on two lines to show their functions in both keys.

	C	Dm	G7	C	B♭	F
C:	I	ii	V7	I		
				F: V	IV	I

EXERCISE 68 🖉

Below the following progressions, write their harmonic analyses.

1. | Fmaj7 | C7 | Fmaj7 | Fmaj7 | A♭maj7 | B♭m7 E♭7
   | A♭maj7 | A♭maj7 ||

2. | E | C#m | A | B | D | G | D | A ||

3. | A | C#m | D | A | F#m | B7 | E ||

4. | Dm | C | B♭ | A | Dsus4 | D | Em | G | D ||

5. | Am7♭5 | D7 | Gm | B♭7 | E♭ | Fm7 | Gm7 | A♭ ||

Transposition

To make a song fit a singer's vocal range, sometimes it's necessary to *transpose* it, moving the melody and all of the chords in the same direction by the same interval. The use of numbers to identify chord functions and scale degrees eases the job of transposition.

Here is a chord progression in the key of B♭. To prepare to transpose it to any key, first we write the harmonic analysis with the numeric function of each chord below its letter name.

$\frac{3}{4}$ B♭	Dm	Cm	Cm	F	F	B♭		F7	
I	iii	ii			V	I		V7	

‖ B♭	B♭	Cm	Cm	F	F	E♭		B♭	
I		ii			V	IV		I	

B♭	B♭	Cm	Cm	F	F	E♭ F E♭/G	F Gm F/A
I		ii			V	IV V IV	V vi V

B♭	Dm	Cm	C	F	F	B♭		F7	‖
I	iii	ii	II		V	I		V	

B♭	B♭	Cm	Cm	F	F	E♭		B♭	
I		ii			V	IV		I	

B♭	B♭	Cm	Cm	F	F	E♭ F E♭/G	F Gm F/A
I		ii			V	IV V IV	V vi V

B♭	Dm	Cm	C	F	F	B♭		F7	B♭ ‖
I	iii	ii	II		V	I		V	I

Let's say the original version is too high for the singer, and we want to transpose the song down one-and-a-half steps to the key of G. We review the diatonic chords in the key, based on the G major scale.

G	Am	Bm	C	D7	Em	F♯m7♭5
I	ii	iii	IV	V	vi	vii

Now we apply the new chords to the numeric progression of the song.

```
|¾ G  | Bm | Am | Am | D | D | G      | D7    |
|  I  | iii | ii |    | V | I | V7     |

|| G  | G  | Am | Am | D | D | C      | G     |
|  I  |    | ii |    | V |   | IV     | I     |

| G   | G  | Am | Am | D | D | C D C/E | D Em D/F♯ |
|  I  |    | ii |    | V |   | IV V IV | V vi V    |

| G   | Bm | Am | A  | D | D | G       | D    ||
|  I  | iii| ii | II | V | I | V       |

| G   | G  | Am | Am | D | D | C       | G    |
|  I  |    | ii |    | V |   | IV      | I    |

| G   | G  | Am | Am | D | D | C D C/E | D Em D/F♯ |
|  I  |    | ii |    | V |   | IV V IV | V vi V    |

| G   | Bm | Am | A  | D | D | G       | D    | G    ||
|  I  | iii| ii | II | V | I | V       |      | I    |
```

EXERCISE 69 🖉

Transpose the progression on page 101 to the key of E♭.

FORM

Knowing the form of a song helps us to effectively memorize and interpret it. Sections of songs are most commonly eight, twelve, or sixteen measures long.

Blues Forms

Blues progressions are hidden within songs in other styles, so it's important to know them. The most common is the *12-bar* blues form; it follows the general chord progression below, which you should memorize and learn in other keys. Once you are familiar with this basic form, you can learn to recognize its many variations.

I	I	I	I
IV	IV	I	I
V	IV	I	I

The final two measures of the blues progression often contain a *turnaround*, a short progression designed to push us back to the top. This example has a typical turnaround: I–IV–I–V.

	I	I	I	I	I
IV	IV	I	I	I
V	IV	I	IV	I	V	I

Here is a typical *8-bar* blues form; one of many variants.

|I|V|IV|IV|
|I|V|I|V|

The blues progression may consist of only major or minor triads or dominant chords on the numbers shown on the previous page, or it may be dressed up with extra chord changes. The overall structure and general sense of harmonic movement remains.

EXERCISE 70 🖉

Write and play the 12-bar blues progression, with the I–IV–I–V turnaround, in the keys of F, B♭, G, and D.

Other Forms

Popular song forms often use three main sections: the *chorus*, the *verse*, and a *bridge*. After a possible introduction, either a verse or a chorus may start the tune. Usually the chorus contains the catchiest part of the song (the *hook*) and a strong chord move or resolution. The chorus often includes the song title in the lyrics as well.

The verses usually start at a lower energy level and provide supporting material for and build up to the chorus. Typically the verse contains fewer chord changes and a lower dynamic (volume) level than the chorus, and the lyrics provide additional story elements or development of the song's theme.

The main purpose of the bridge is to provide contrast to the other sections, possibly changing keys or the rhythmic feel, along with lyric content that contrasts the other sections.

Multi-sectioned tunes, especially instrumentals, may just use *rehearsal letters* (A, B, C, etc.) to label the sections. The *32-bar* or *AABA* song form is used for many well-known *standards* (songs that stand the test of time). This form consists of four sections, each containing eight measures. Usually the first, second, and final sections (A) are similar in melodic phrasing and chord-progression structure. The B section acts as a bridge, with contrasting material.

EXERCISE 71 🖉

Map out three short pop songs by counting the number of measures in each section and the number of sections in each tune. Write down the basic form, which might look something like this:

Intro (4 bars)

Verse (8 bars)

Chorus (8 bars)

Verse (8 bars)

Chorus (8 bars)

Bridge (10 bars)

Solo Verse (8 bars)

Chorus (8 bars)

Chorus (8 bars)

Ending (8 bars)

Chart Directions

A basic written version of a song may contain chords, the main melody, a few important phrases played by the instruments, and most importantly, the form. This is called a *chart* or a *lead sheet*. On it, you will see symbols and instructions that tell you to repeat sections a specific number of times, or to jump to an end section when you reach a specific measure. These symbols make the chart shorter, requiring less writing by the copyist and less page-turning by the player.

Instead of specifying every note, we can notate chord attacks and durations with *rhythm slashes* that cross the center of the staff. Diamond shapes indicate whole-note chords.

Repeat signs tell you to play everything between them twice. A right-facing repeat sign must always be followed by a left-facing one. Another handy symbol is the one-bar repeat (𝄎).

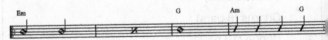

If there is only a left-facing repeat sign, repeat from the very beginning.

You may use instructions such as *Play 3 times* over a repeated section. Be sure **not** to use the vague direction *Repeat 2 times* when writing your charts.

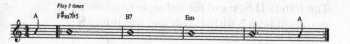

Numbered Endings

Often a repeated section has a different phrase at the end of each iteration. Keep track of how many times you have played the section and go to the appropriate ending each time. Follow the numbers written below the staff to see how it works. Each time through, you are required to play one ending only, skipping over the previously-played endings.

Italian Directions

The letters **D.C.** stand for the Italian *da capo*, meaning *from the head*. This means to immediately return to and play from the beginning of the piece. After following a **D.C.**, it's customary to ignore all repeat signs you've already encountered, playing only the final numbered ending(s), unless you were directed otherwise in a phrase such as **D.C. w/ repeats** or **repeats good**.

Eventually you will play up to the **D.C.** mark again. This time, ignore it! It only applies once.

The letters **D.S.** stand for *dal segno* (*from the sign*). The sign itself is an S with a slash and two dots (𝄋).

Before playing the song, make a mental note of the location of the sign and the letters **D.S.** on the chart. The sign will always be well before the **D.S.** Play past the sign the first time through; it will be a starting place later. When you finally arrive at the letters **D.S.**, jump back to the sign without stopping and continue to play. The rule regarding previous repeated sections after following a **D.S.** is the same as for a **D.C.**: they're usually ignored. Take any final numbered ending.

Either **D.C.** or **D.S.** may be accompanied by the instruction **al Fine** (pronounced *feenay*), literally meaning *to the end*. The word **Fine** will appear later in the music. After jumping to the beginning (**D.C.**) or to the sign (**D.S.**), continue playing and stop when you arrive at the word **Fine**.

Instead of **al Fine**, you may see **al Coda** (meaning *to the tail*), referring to an extra section of music used as an ending. The coda symbol looks like the crosshairs on a rifle scope.

As with the *segno*, do nothing but make a mental note of the locations of the coda symbols the first time you see them. After following the instruction to jump to the beginning (**D.C.**) or to the sign (**D.S.**), continue playing until you arrive at the first coda symbol. Then, without stopping, jump to the other coda-marked section near the end.

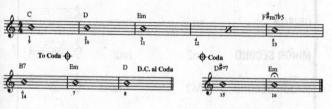

Before starting to play, always take a few seconds to find all of the chart directions and talk through or mentally follow the path they indicate through the chart. If there is confusion, ask the bandleader about the form.

TABLES

Intervals

INTERVAL	ABBREVIATION	STEPS	PITCHES
UNISON	unis	none	
MINOR SECOND	m2	half	
MAJOR SECOND	M2	whole	
AUGMENTED SECOND	aug2	1 1/2	
MINOR THIRD	m3	1 1/2	
MAJOR THIRD	M3	2	
PERFECT FOURTH	P4	2 1/2	
AUGMENTED FOURTH	aug4	3	
DIMINISHED FIFTH	dim5	3	
PERFECT FIFTH	P5	3 1/2	
AUGMENTED FIFTH	aug5	4	
MINOR SIXTH	m6	4	

INTERVAL	ABBREVIATION	STEPS	PITCHES
MAJOR SIXTH	M6	4 1/2	
AUGMENTED SIXTH	aug6	5	
MINOR SEVENTH	m7	5	
MAJOR SEVENTH	M7	5 1/2	
PERFECT OCTAVE	P8	6	
MINOR NINTH	m9	6 1/2	
MAJOR NINTH	M9	7	
AUGMENTED NINTH	aug9	7 1/2	
PERFECT ELEVENTH	P11	8 1/2	
AUGMENTED ELEVENTH	aug11	9	
MINOR THIRTEENTH	m13	10 1/2	
MAJOR THIRTEENTH	M13	11	

Scale Construction

SCALE	TONE NUMBERS
MAJOR	1-2-3-4-5-6-7
NATURAL MINOR	1-2-b3-4-5-b6-b7
MAJOR PENTATONIC	1-2-3-5-6
MINOR PENTATONIC	1-b3-4-5-b7
BLUES	1-b3-4-b5-5-b7
MAJOR BLUES	1-2-b3-3-4-b5-5-6-b7
MINOR BLUES	1-2-b3-4-b5-5-b6-b7
IONIAN MODE (major)	1-2-3-4-5-6-7
DORIAN MODE	1-2-b3-4-5-6-b7
PHRYGIAN MODE	1-b2-b3-4-5-b6-b7
LYDIAN MODE	1-2-3-#4-5-6-7
MIXOLYDIAN MODE	1-2-3-4-5-6-b7
AEOLIAN MODE (nat. minor)	1-2-b3-4-5-b6-b7
LOCRIAN MODE	1-b2-b3-4-b5-b6-b7
HARMONIC MINOR	1-2-b3-4-5-b6-7
PHRYGIAN DOMINANT (Spanish)	1-b2-3-4-5-b6-b7
JAZZ MELODIC MINOR	1-2-b3-4-5-6-7
DORIAN b2	1-b2-b3-4-5-6-b7
LYDIAN AUGMENTED	1-2-3-#4-#5-6-7
LYDIAN b7	1-2-3-#4-5-6-b7
MIXOLYDIAN b13 (Hindu)	1-2-3-4-5-b6-b7
LOCRIAN #2	1-2-b3-4-b5-b6-b7
SUPER LOCRIAN (Altered)	1-b2-b3-b4-b5-b6-b7
CHROMATIC	1-b2-2-b3-3-4-b5-5-b6-6-b7-7
WHOLE TONE	1-2-3-#4-#5-#6
DIMINISHED WHOLE HALF	1-2-b3-4-b5-b6-6-7
DIMINISHED HALF WHOLE	1-b2-b3-b4-b5-5-6-b7
HUNGARIAN MINOR	1-2-b3-#4-5-b6-7
DOUBLE HARMONIC	1-b2-3-4-5-b6-7
ENIGMATIC	1-b2-3-#4-#5-#6-7
JAPANESE	1-b2-4-5-b6

INTERVAL STRUCTURE

W-W-H-W-W-W-H
W-H-W-W-H-W-W

W-W-W+H-W-W+H
W+H-W-W-W+H-W
W+H-W-H-H-W+H-W
W-H-H-H-H-H-W-H-W
W-H-W-H-H-H-W-W

W-W-H-W-W-W-H
W-H-W-W-W-H-W
H-W-W-W-H-W-W
W-W-H-W-W-W-H
W-W-H-W-W-H-W
W-H-W-W-W-W-W
H-W-W-H-W-W-W

W-H-W-W-H-W+H-H
H-W+H-H-W-H-W-W

W-H-W-W-W-W-H
H-W-W-W-W-H-W
W-W-W-W-H-W-H
W-W-W-H-W-H-W
W-W-H-W-H-W-W
W-H-W-H-W-W-W
H-W-H-W-W-W-W

H-H-H-H-H-H-H-H-H-H-H-H
W-W-W-W-W-W
W-H-W-H-W-H-W-H
H-W-H-W-H-W-H-W

W-H-W+H-H-W-H+H-H
H-W+H-H-W-H-W-H+H-H
H-W+H-W-W-W-W-H-H
H-W+H-W-H-W-H+H

Chord Construction

CHORD TYPE	FORMULA
MAJOR	1-3-5
FIFTH (POWER CHORD)	1-5
SUSPENDED FOURTH	1-4-5
SUSPENDED SECOND	1-2-5
ADDED NINTH	1-3-5-9
SIXTH	1-3-5-6
SIXTH, ADDED NINTH	1-3-5-6-9
MAJOR SEVENTH	1-3-5-7
MAJOR NINTH	1-3-5-7-9
MAJOR SEVENTH, SHARP ELEVENTH	1-3-5-7-#11
MAJOR THIRTEENTH	1-3-5-7-9-13
MINOR	1-♭3-5
MINOR, ADDED NINTH	1-♭3-5-9
MINOR SIXTH	1-♭3-5-6
MINOR, FLAT SIXTH	1-♭3-5-♭6
MINOR SIXTH, ADDED NINTH	1-♭3-5-6-9
MINOR SEVENTH	1-♭3-5-♭7
MINOR SEVENTH, FLAT FIFTH	1-♭3-♭5-♭7
MINOR, MAJOR SEVENTH	1-♭3-5-7
MINOR NINTH	1-♭3-5-♭7-9
MINOR NINTH, FLAT FIFTH	1-♭3-♭5-♭7-9
MINOR NINTH, MAJOR SEVENTH	1-♭3-5-7-9
MINOR ELEVENTH	1-♭3-5-♭7-9-11
MINOR THIRTEENTH	1-♭3-5-♭7-9-11-13

NOTES	CHORD NAME
C-E-G	C
C-G	C5
C-F-G	Csus4
C-D-G	Csus2
C-E-G-D	Cadd9
C-E-G-A	C6
C-E-G-A-D	C6/9
C-E-G-B	Cmaj7
C-E-G-B-D	Cmaj9
C-E-G-B-F♯	Cmaj7♯11
C-E-G-B-D-A	Cmaj13
C-E♭-G	Cm
C-E♭-G-D	Cm(add9)
C-E♭-G-A	Cm6
C-E♭-G-A♭	Cm♭6
C-Eb-G-A-D	Cm6/9
C-E♭-G-B♭	Cm7
C-E♭-G♭-B♭	Cm7♭5
C-E♭-G-B	Cm(maj7)
C-E♭-G-B♭-D	Cm9
C-E♭-G♭-B♭-D	Cm9♭5
C-E♭-G-B-D	Cm9(maj7)
C-E♭-G-B♭-D-F	Cm11
C-E♭-G-B♭-D-F-A	Cm13

CHORD TYPE	FORMULA
DOMINANT SEVENTH	1-3-5-♭7
SEVENTH, SUSPENDED FOURTH	1-4-5-♭7
SEVENTH, FLAT FIFTH	1-3-♭5-♭7
NINTH	1-3-5-♭7-9
NINTH, SUSPENDED FOURTH	1-4-5-♭7-9
NINTH, FLAT FIFTH	1-3-♭5-♭7-9
SEVENTH, FLAT NINTH	1-3-5-♭7-♭9
SEVENTH, SHARP NINTH	1-3-5-♭7-♯9
SEVENTH, FLAT FIFTH, SHARP NINTH	1-3-♭5-♭7-♯9
ELEVENTH	1-5-♭7-9-11
SEVENTH, SHARP ELEVENTH	1-3-5-♭7-♯11
THIRTEENTH	1-3-5-♭7-9-13
THIRTEENTH, SUSPENDED FOURTH	1-4-5-♭7-9-13
AUGMENTED	1-3-♯5
SEVENTH, SHARP FIFTH	1-3-♯5-♭7
NINTH, SHARP FIFTH	1-3-♯5-♭7-9
SEVENTH, SHARP FIFTH, FLAT NINTH	1-3-♯5-♭7-♭9
SEVENTH, SHARP FIFTH, SHARP NINTH	1-3-♯5-♭7-♯9
DIMINISHED	1-♭3-♭5
DIMINISHED SEVENTH	1-♭3-♭5-♭♭7

NOTES	CHORD NAME
C-E-G-B♭	C7
C-F-G-B♭	C7sus4
C-E-G♭-B♭	C7♭5
C-E-G-B♭-D	C9
C-F-G-B♭-D	C9sus4
C-E-G♭-B♭-D	C9♭5
C-E-G-B♭-D♭	C7♭9
C-E-G-B♭-D♯	C7♯9
C-E-G♭-B♭-D♯	C7♭5(♯9)
C-G-B♭-D-F	C11
C-E-G-B♭-F♯	C7♯11
C-E-G-B♭-D-A	C13
C-F-G-B♭-D-A	C13sus4
C-E-G♯	Caug
C-E-G♯-B♭	Caug7
C-E-G♯-B♭-D	Caug9
C-E-G♯-B♭-D♭	Caug7♭9
C-E-G♯-B♭-D♯	Caug7♯9
C-E♭-G♭	Cdim
C-E♭-G♭-B♭♭	Cdim7

ANSWER KEY

EXERCISE 7

A E B C D B D B

EXERCISE 8

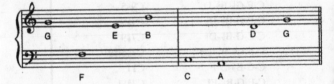

G E B D G

F C A

EXERCISE 12

EXERCISE 13

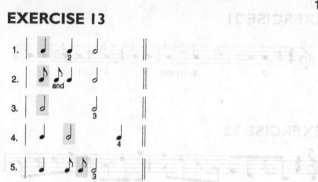

EXERCISE 14

EXERCISE 15

EXERCISE 20

EXERCISE 21

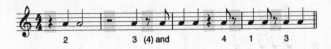

EXERCISE 22

EXERCISE 23

EXERCISE 24

121

EXERCISE 25

EXERCISE 26

EXERCISE 28

EXERCISE 31

A E E♭ D E♭ C   A E E C C♯   C♯ A A C   A E G G♯ A G♯ A

EXERCISE 34

1. F# minor
2. D minor
3. G minor
4. B minor
5. D# minor
6. E minor
7. C minor
8. C# minor
9. A minor
10. G# minor

EXERCISE 35

1. G major
2. Db major
3. F major
4. E major
5. Ab major
6. D major
7. Bb major
8. B major
9. Eb major
10. C major

EXERCISE 36

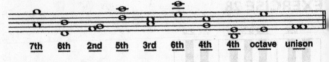

7th   6th   2nd   5th   3rd   6th   4th   4th   octave   unison

EXERCISE 37

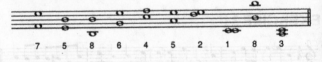

7   5   8   6   4   5   2   1   8   3

EXERCISE 38

P4   maj3   maj6   maj2   P5

maj7   P8   maj6   P5   maj3

EXERCISE 39

min6   dim5   maj2   min7   aug4

min3   min6   dim8   maj6   maj7

EXERCISE 40

dim5   maj2   min7   maj6   aug4

min3   P5   min2   dim7   min6

EXERCISE 41

maj3　　P4　　min7　　min7　　aug5

P5　　min7　　maj2　　min3　　maj6

EXERCISE 43

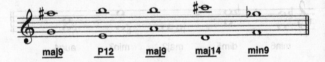

maj9　　P12　　maj9　　maj14　　min9

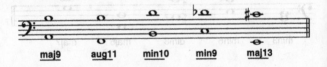

maj9　　aug11　　min10　　min9　　maj13

EXERCISE 44

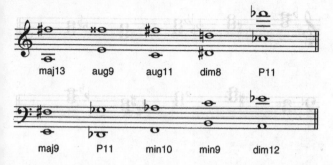

maj13   aug9   aug11   dim8   P11

maj9   P11   min10   min9   dim12

EXERCISE 46

EXERCISE 47

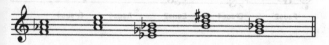

EXERCISE 48

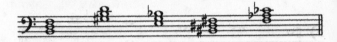

EXERCISE 49

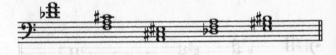

EXERCISE 50

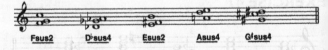

Fsus2   D♭sus4   Esus2   Asus4   G♯sus4

EXERCISE 51

Esus4 Absus2 D#sus4 G#sus4 C#sus2

Gsus4 Dbsus2 Asus4 Fsus2 Bsus4

EXERCISE 52

Eb/G	E/B	Ab/Cb	Db/F	B/F#
1st inv.	2nd inv.	1st inv.	1st inv.	2nd inv.

G/D	Dm/A	A/C#	F/C	Bb/F
2nd inv.	2nd inv.	1st inv.	2nd inv.	2nd inv.

EXERCISE 53

EXERCISE 54

EXERCISE 57

EXERCISE 61

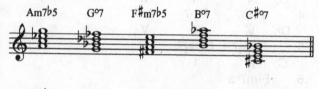

EXERCISE 64

1.　　Fmaj7　　Dm7　　C7
　　F:　I　　　　vi　　　V

2.　　C#m7　　F#m7
　　A:　iii　　　vi
　　E:　vi　　　　ii

3.　　Am7　　Cmaj7　　Em7
　　C:　vi　　I　　　　iii
　　G:　ii　　IV　　　vi

4.　　B♭m7　　Fm7　　A♭7
　　D♭:　vi　　iii　　　V

5.　　Fmaj7　　Cmaj7
　　C:　IV　　　I

6.　　F#m7♭5
　　G:　vii°

7.　　Em7　　F#m7　　A7
　　D:　ii　　iii　　　V

8.　　G#m7　　C#m7　　Emaj7
　　E:　iii　　vi　　　I
　　B:　vi　　　ii　　　IV

9.　　Fm7　　B♭7
　　E♭:　ii　　V

10.　A♭maj7　Cm7　　D♭maj7
　　A♭:　I　　　iii　　　IV

EXERCISE 65

1.   Dm   G   C
  C: ii   V   I

2.   D   Bm   G   A
  D: I   vi   IV   V

3.   D   Em   G
  D: I   ii   IV
  G: V   vi   I

4.   D   E   F#m   G#°
  A: IV   V   vi   vii°

5.   C#m   A   E
  A: iii   I   V
  E: vi   IV   I

6.   F   B♭   Dm
  F: I   IV   vi
  B♭:   V   I   iii

7.   E♭   Cm
  E♭:   I   vi
  A♭:   V   iii
  B♭:   IV   ii

8.   B♭m   D♭   A♭
  D♭:   vi   I   V
  A♭:   ii   IV   I

9.   G   D   C   G
  G: I   V   IV   I

10.   A   F#m   E
  A: I   vi   V
  E: IV   ii   I

EXERCISE 66

1. | Dm7♭5 | G7 | Cm7 | Fm7
Cm: | iim7♭5 | V7 | im7 | ivm7

2. | Em | D7 | Am | B7
Em: | i | ♭VII7 | iv | V7

3. | Fm7 | E♭7 | D♭maj7 | C7
Fm: | im7 | ♭VII7 | ♭VImaj7 | V7
G: | V | vi | I |

4. | Em | Bm | Am |
Em: | i | v | iv |

5. | Gm | B♭ | Cm | D7
Gm: | i | ♭III | iv | V7

6. | Am7 | Dm7 | Bm7♭5 | E7
Am: | im7 | ivm7 | iim7♭5 | V7

7. | F | C7 | B♭maj7 | Dm
Dm: | ♭III | ♭VII | ♭VImaj7 | i

8. | B♭m | A♭ | D♭ | F7
B♭m: | i | ♭VII | ♭III | V7

9. | Cm | Gm | E♭ | A♭
Cm: | i | v | ♭III | ♭VI

10. | F♯m | E | A | C♯7
F♯m: | i | ♭VII | ♭III | V7

EXERCISE 68

1. Fmaj7| C7 |Fmaj7|Fmaj7| A♭maj7| B♭m7E♭7 |A♭maj7 | A♭maj7 ||
  F: Imaj7 V7 Imaj7   A♭:Imaj7   iim7 V7 Imaj7

2. E | C#m | A | B | D | G | D | A ||
  E: I   vi   IV V
                  D: I   IV   I   V

3. A | C#m | D | A | F#m | B7 | E ||
  A: I   iii   IV I   vi
               E: ii   V7   I

4. Dm | C | B♭ | A | Dsus4 | D | Em | G | D ||
  Dm: i ♭VII ♭VI V
               D: V   I   I ii IV I

5. Am7♭5 | D7 | Gm | B♭7 | E♭ | Fm7 | Gm7 | A♭ ||
  Gm:iim7♭5 V7   i
               E♭: iii   V   I   iim7 iiim7 IV